Blessed Among Women

Peter de Rosa

Blessed Among Women
THE BOOK OF MARY

the columba press

First published in 2005 by

the columba press

55A Spruce Avenue, Stillorgan Industrial Park,
Blackrock, Co Dublin.

Cover by Bill Bolger
Origination by The Columba Press
Printed in Ireland by ColourBooks Ltd, Dublin

ISBN 1 85607 481 1

Acknowledgements

Modern poems and translations not attributed in the text
are the author's copyright. The publisher has failed to trace
copyright holders in a few other quoted materials, and we
invite such copyright holders to contact us so that matters
can be put right.

Contents

Introduction

Think of this book as one long hymn of praise to Mary, the Virgin Mother of God. In the finest Christian poem ever written, 'The Divine Comedy', Dante is about to be ushered into the divine presence when he is told by his guide:

First look upon the face
That most resembles Christ's
For only the beauty of her face
Can prepare thee to see
The face of Christ.

In her innocence, Mary seems younger than a new-born babe and, in her wisdom, older than the stars. The Catholic instinct is to look on her face first, not because she is above Christ but because she is his Mother and ours, too. As the Irish say, mothers do not come in twos and threes. As our spiritual mother, Mary is unique. It would be impossible to imagine the world without her.

This book is divided into two parts, *Devotion* and *Reflection*. In it you will see how Mary has been honoured in the past and is honoured still. There was a time when a thousand plants and flowers were named after her, when the finest buildings ever constructed in Europe, the French cathedrals, were dedicated to her. Columbus sailed from the Old World with his flag-ship named *Santa Maria* as if to say that the New World was hers to conquer, too.

The conquest began in earnest in 1531 when Mary appeared to a Mexican-Indian woodcutter named Juan Diego on the hill of Tepeyac, just north of Mexico City. She spoke in the Náhuatl (Aztec) language and identified herself by the name of Guadalupe. She left her image on Juan's poncho, not that of a European but of a dark-skinned native woman, silhouetted in sunlight and standing on a crescent moon. Thus she began the spread of Christianity throughout the continent.

Our Lady of Guadalupe, Patron of the Americas, inspired Mexicans to fight for independence from Spain in the early 19th century. In the 1960s, she gave farmworkers the courage to demand their rights.

In our own day, it is a remarkable fact that Mary's humble shrines across the world attract more visitors than Disneyland and Disneyworld combined.

This book shows how Mary helps us cope with the problems of life – sickness, hunger and thirst, failure, despair, bereavement, loneliness. Psychoanalyst Carl Jung thinks of Mary as the Sophia (or Wisdom) that is of God. She stands by mankind as its friend and advocate with God. She reveals, he says, 'the bright side, the kind, just and friendly side of God'. This is why she is our Peace.

Ave Domus Pacis
God's own House of Peace
When you look upon our sorrows
They all cease.

She is by our side when our dear ones die. Many Christians pray thousands of times that, in the hour of their own death, she will take care of them. In the words of an ancient Irish poem:

O Mary, our Mother, lead us home.

O Mary, when our eyes close in our last sleep,

and open to behold thy Son, the just judge,

and the Angel opens the Book,

and the Enemy accuses us,

in that terrible hour, come to our aid,

be with us.

In Part One, you are invited to dip in and out of these pages looking for, say, a favourite prayer or poem, carol or hymn. Among the carols is the first ever written on the North American continent. Some poems, dating back over a thousand years, have been newly translated. Others have been written specially for this book.

There are chapters on Mary's many titles, on the Rosary, on the way Ireland has stayed faithful to this great Marian devotion and helped spread it from the old world to the Americas. Another chapter deals with the many Black Madonnas which have been preserved in Catholic churches and cathedrals.

In Part Two, you will see that Mary is honoured not only among Catholics like St Francis of Assisi and Cardinal Newman but among Orthodox Christians of the East. It may surprise many readers that she is revered, too, by great Protestants like Martin Luther, as well as by Muslims, beginning with their Prophet Mohammed. As Pope John Paul II has often said, Mary will play a key role in Christian reunion and in friendship with other faiths.

Marian devotion has many facets to it but to summarise them very simply:

Jesus says,
'By their fruits you shall know them,'
and, 'Go and bear fruit,
fruit that remains,
so that whatever you ask the Father
in my name, he will give it you.'

Mary is the woman who bore God's Son;
her Fruit remains for ever.

She it was who bowed her head at the words,
'Blessed is the fruit of thy womb.'

She is, therefore, the one whose prayers
are always answered.

This single idea implicitly contains
the whole of Christian thinking
about Mary through the ages.
This is why she is
blessed among women.

PART ONE

Devotion

1. In Praise of Mary

Frank Cappa's movie, *It's a Wonderful Life*, tells the story of George Bailey (James Stewart), the selfless hero of Bedford Falls. George, a married man with two children, reaches the point of thinking the world would be better off without him.

While he is contemplating suicide, his guardian angel appears. Clarence is no angel by Fra Angelico. As a beginner, he has no wings and he's disguised as a bumbling white-haired old man.

George is about to jump off a bridge when Clarence jumps in, forcing the good-hearted George to jump in after him and save him.

Clarence sets about showing George how valuable he is. To do this, he grants him one wish: to see what life would be like if he had never been born. In this alternate world, his wife Mary (played by Donna Reed) is a lonely old maid. His brother is dead because George was not there to save him from drowning. His inebriate uncle Billy is in a mental home. The local greedy villain, without George to oppose him, owns the whole town.

Finally realising how much good he has done, how rich he is in love and friendship, George asks to be allowed to live again, and God grants his wish.

Mary's Angel, Gabriel, far more polished than Clarence, does not say to her, 'You have conceived in your womb.' No, everything is in the future tense: 'You will conceive and bear a son … the Holy Spirit will come upon you, the child to be born of you will be called holy, the Son of God.'

The future was still open. Mary was free. She could have said No, or there would have been no merit in her response. But grasping what the world would be like if she did say No – no overshadowing of the Holy Spirit, no Son of God, no Kingdom come – she says, 'Be it done unto me according to thy Word.' Immediately the impossible becomes possible; a new world has begun.

Since this book is a hymn of praise to Mary the Immaculate Virgin Mother of God, first try to imagine an alternate world without her. So many beautiful things would not exist – apart from Jesus of Nazareth!

We would lose the paintings of the Madonna by Leonardo and Raphael, Murillo, and Fra Angelico.

No Bach's *Magnificat*, no Benjamin Britten's *Hymn to the Virgin*, none of the music dedicated to her by Bruchner and Rachmaninov, no *Ave Maria* by Schubert which, he instantly noted, 'grips every soul and turns it to devotion'.

We would have no Marian poetry by Rilke, Chesterton, or Gerard Manley Hopkins.

The great anti-slavery novel *Uncle Tom's Cabin* would not have been written had not Harriet Beecher Stowe been inspired by Mary's *Magnificat*.

Without Mary, there would be none of the inspiring prayers to her, no hymns or carols in her honour, no festivals of Christmas or Easter, no statues such as Epstein's *Madonna and Child* or Michelangelo's *Pietà*, no great cathedrals of Chartres, Milan and Notre Dame in Paris, which are poetry in stone.

Without her compassion many parents would be comfortless when their sons and daughters are taken from them in the flower of their youth. A poem by an unknown Greek called 'A Prayer' delicately expresses Mary's silent compassion.

> He was a sailor lad whom the deep sea took.
> His mother, unsuspecting, moves to light
> A tall candle before the Blessed Virgin
> For blue skies and his swift return,
> As always hearkening to the wind.
> And while she prays and prays,
> The Icon watches her, sad and solemn, knowing
> That the boy she waits for
> Will never come home.

Without the example of her chaste goodness, many women would probably still be chattels of men.

Without her by their side, many mothers would find it harder to endure the pains of childbirth, many men, women and children would die friendless and afraid. Hilaire Belloc's poem 'In a Boat' expresses their dependence on her:

Mother of God
And Mother of me.
Save me alive
From the howl of the sea.

Mary is like a great river running through the church like the Mississippi in America or the Danube in Europe that fashioned communities, trade and culture along their banks. Remove Mary and there would be a huge gap in Western civilisation that nothing could fill.

When Jesus was in Bethany in the house of Simon the leper, a woman anointed his head with costly ointment as he sat at table. When his disciples muttered about the waste, Jesus said, 'She has done a beautiful thing to me … Truly, I say to you, wherever this gospel is preached in the whole world, what she has done will be told in memory of her' (Mt 26:10,13). If such a simple act was worth remembering for ever, how much more worth remembering is the mothering Jesus received from Mary?

In her own person, she fulfilled all St Paul's tests of charity. She embodied all the beatitudes. She was meek and lowly, she was perfectly pure, she suffered as no other has done for justice's sake as she watched her Son die in shame on the cross.

An amusing old story tells of Jesus saying to the crowd intent on stoning to death the woman taken in adultery, 'Let whoever is without sin throw the first stone.' When a stone is flung from the back of the crowd, Jesus looks up and sighs, 'Not you, Mother.' However, the point of the gospel story is, sinners shouldn't throw stones; the sinless, like Jesus and Mary, cannot. Mary always stands on the side of the sinner and the lost.

To French writer Georges Bernanos, while Mary is a queen, she is still a little girl. Since she knew nothing of sin, her eyes are the only real 'child-eyes' since the beginning of the race. In that sense, she is 'younger than the race from which she sprang' and, though a mother by grace, she is our youngest sister. Maybe this is why when St Teresa of Avila had a vision of Mary she looked 'almost like a child' and why in all her major apparitions at, say, Lourdes and Fatima, Mary is eternally young.

Matthew and Luke imply she was not merely a virgin but dedicated to virginity. This meant that she was the only Jewish woman who was essentially unable to give birth to the Messiah. Yet, in God's providence, she did so. Even then, she risked being stoned to death for adultery, since the child was not her husband's. No wonder Christians praise her for her courage and child-like innocence.

Bells of all sizes in town and country ring out her praises. ('And every note of every bell/ Sang Gabriel! Rang Gabriel!') Millions of Aves praise her each day, fulfilling her own prophecy that all generations would call her blessed. And, of course, countless legends grew up around her.

In a homily on Corpus Christi 1964, St Josemaría recalled one of the songs collected by Spanish King Alfonso X. 'It's a legend about a simple monk who begged Our Lady to let him see heaven, even if only for a moment. Our Lady granted him his wish and the good monk found himself in paradise. When he returned, he could not recognise the monastery – his prayer, which he had thought very short, lasted three centuries. Three centuries are nothing to a person in love.'

Mary is deeply embedded in our culture. Medieval cathedrals were the spas and hospitals of the day at a time when faith and prayer were the only therapies. The sick flocked to them, seeking Mary's help as they once brought their needs to Jesus in the Holy Land. 'Mother of Mercy' was the ceaseless cry of the old, the blind, the lame, and their loyal helpers. 'Mother of Mercy' echoed day and night in the cathedrals and their precincts. Whenever there was a rumour of a cure numbers multiplied, swelling 'Mother of Mercy' to a giant chorus of love and longing.

At Christmas, thousands of people used to walk for weeks to the nearest cathedral to celebrate midnight Mass. There they stayed through that night and the next morning, soaking up music, light and beauty into lives otherwise full of back-breaking labour and misery.

Today those cathedrals continue to provide sanctuary for those with modern ills – loneliness, frustration, the sense of alienation.

French writer Léon Bloy pictured heaven as a Garden of Paradise, its dew the faithful's tears. 'Then the sun will rise like a pale Byzantine Virgin in the golden mosaic, and the earth will waken and scatter her scents.'

When, in his *Divine Comedy*, Dante reached heaven, the first hymn he heard was the *Ave Maria*, a song that brought serenity to the faces of the angelic host.

For 15 centuries, not one Mass has been said by Roman or Greek Christians without her being praised as our intercessor with her Son. This is why we honour her as advocate and co-redeemer.

Without her, we would not have salvation because we would not have Jesus. Christianity is a religion of incarnation which means a religion of Mother and Child. Jesus did not appear fully grown out of thin air, out of nowhere, like Adam in the Genesis story. He was 'born of a woman' (Gal 4:4). He was the fruit of a woman's body (Lk 1:42). If he were not, he would not be a member of the human race at all, not a child of Adam but a completely new species.

As soon as God's Son was born, like any child, he was put in the arms of his mother and bonded with her. That bonding was instantaneous and life-long. Without her, we dare to say, Jesus would have little appeal, for he would be an outsider, a stranger.

The Prophet Isaiah said:
> All flesh is as grass,
> It's beauty will pass,
> As in a field the flowers do.
> The grasses grow pale
> And the flowers fail,
> Frail as the flowers are you.

Mary provided Jesus with the frail flesh he needed to save the world. According to Luke, he began his work in his mother's womb through the sound of her voice. Elizabeth says, 'Behold, when the voice of your greeting came to my ears, the babe in my womb leaped for joy' (1:45).

In art, Jesus was originally depicted not as the Risen One, nor as the Crucified, nor even as a new-born babe, but as a child on his mother's lap. This is why she was called *Sedes Sapientiae*, the Seat of Wisdom. In the first representation of Jesus, dating from the 2nd century, he is in his mother's arms as he is greeted by the Magi, Easterners, Gentiles, as if to say Mary's child is the Saviour of all.

The humblest things reminded them of her. For instance, the strawberry. 'Doubtless God could have made a better berry,' wrote William Butler, 'but doubtless God never did.'

Medieval artists portrayed the Virgin Mary with strawberries, the perfect fruit. In her honour, craftsmen carved them on church altars and around the capitals of cathedral pillars. Mary was often painted as 'The Madonna of the Strawberries'. Some artists put in the entire plant with its red fruit and white blossom.

Monks adorned their tapestries and illuminated manuscripts with them. In a French miniature (c. 1400), Joseph stretches out his hand with a strawberry in it to the child Jesus, coaxing him to take his first step. Another shows Mary with her child on her knee while angels gather strawberries to feed him. In a delightful 15th century drawing by Dührer, entitled 'Mary and the Many Animals', Mary is sitting in a garden surrounded by animals. On her knee, Jesus is reaching out to grasp a strawberry leaf.

When Europeans arrived in the New World, they found reminders of Mary in summer meadows so full of small, crimson strawberries their horses' hooves seemed to be covered with blood. One Dutch colonist wrote, 'The flat-land near the river is covered with strawberries, which grow so plentifully in the fields that one can lie down and eat them.'

So central was Mary to Christianity, from 1170-1752, Europe and Britain – with her American colonies – celebrated new year on 25 March, known as Lady Day. The spring solstice was the day of Mary's Christing. On this day when spring begins to chase winter away, the Yes of the Annunciation marked the moment when the Word was made flesh in her womb and our redemption began. Writing his diaries in the 1660s, Samuel Pepys always switched from the old year to the new on Lady Day.

Tribute was paid to Mary by the devout Catholic J. R. H. Tolkien in his epic *Lord of the Rings*, voted the best book of the 20th century. 'It is,' he said, 'a fundamentally religious and Catholic work.' Since he saw Jesus and Mary as the essence of goodness and innocence, the abiding love of his life was the Eucharist and Our Lady 'upon which,' he said, 'all my own small perception of beauty both in majesty and simplicity is founded'. Few readers may have noticed that the final attempt to destroy the Ring, the symbol of evil, and the Dark Lord (Satan) who had forged it, took place on 25 March, that is, Our Lady's Day.

Persecution cannot sever the faithful's devotion to Mary. The oldest lived-in house in England is Saltford Manor in Somerset. It still has paintings on the wall of Mary and her Son, dating from 1200. But the best proof of all is Mary's Shrine at Walsingham in Norfolk, known as England's Nazareth. After Mary appeared there in 1061, every English King for five centuries made a pilgrimage to honour her.

There the sick were cured by Our Lady's might,

The lame made whole, the blind restored to sight.

In 1538, the House and Priory were destroyed at the order of Henry VIII who had previously been there three times as a barefoot pilgrim. The Virgin's famous statue was taken to London and burned.

A 16th century poet penned this moving 'Lament for Walsingham':

Level, level with the ground
The Towers do lie
Which, with their golden glittering tops,
Once pierced the sky.

Owls now screech where sweetest hymns
Were lately sung,
Toads and serpents have their dens
Where palmers once did throng.

Weep, weep, O Walsingham,
Whose days are night:
Blessings turned to blasphemies,
Holy deed to spite.

> Sin is where Our Lady lately sat,
> And heaven is turned to hell,
> Satan sits where Our Lord held sway,
> Walsingham, O Walsingham – farewell.

In a twist of fortune that would have amazed Henry VIII, in 2003 Walsingham was voted England's National Favourite Spiritual Place.

Mary's presence has influenced our culture more than all the philosophers who ever lived. Why this enthusiastic devotion to Mary?

Because she provided Jesus with the flesh that made him one of us. Within her, like any mother, the umbilical cord carried blood between the embryo and the placenta. She was the original source of the blood he shed for our salvation. She was to him what the city of Florence was to Michelangelo, 'the nest wherein I was born'.

If Jesus is the Way, the Truth and the Life, Mary is the way to the Way, the first Yes of recognition to the Truth, the life that gave birth to the Life. In medieval statues, Mary is shown with a book (or scroll) in her hand, possibly of the Jewish Bible. In many paintings of the time, Jesus is sitting on Mary's lap while she holds a book, suggesting that she helped him grasp his destiny inscribed in the Old Testament. Roger van Weyden's picture, 'Virgin and Child' (1450), in which Jesus is tearing a page out of a book, probably symbolises the same thing.

While it's unlikely that in those days a Jewish woman was able to read, the truth behind the imagery is valid: as a mother, Mary instructed the great Teacher. She taught the Word of God to speak, the Son of God to pray, the Messiah to sacrifice himself for love.

An anonymous 15th century Welsh poem says:

Good was the maid, hope's dwelling,
Her flesh bore heaven for you.

Some non-Catholic Christians say that devotion to Mary has no basis in the Bible. With genuine respect, it has to be said they could not be more wrong. In Luke's gospel, Mary was Jesus' first disciple, the first to believe in him, the first Christian. She was first in the most important sense that without her there would have been no second Christian, let alone the millions who throughout history have believed in him.

Mary's belief is far more the church's foundation than St Peter's. When Peter confessed, 'Thou art the Christ the Son of the living God,' Jesus replied, 'Flesh and blood hath not revealed this to thee but my Father who is in heaven.' But without Mary's act of faith, there would have been no Christ for Peter to believe in and, therefore, no kingdom of God and no church.

At the Annunciation, Mary, unlike Peter, had not heard Jesus preach or seen his miracles and yet, already saved, she instantly believed. It was not flesh and blood that revealed the incarnation to her but the living God himself.

In his poem, 'Ave Maria Gratia Plena', Oscar Wilde is puzzled by the coming of Christ. He would have expected to have seen some great God arrive in a rain of gold or God's clear body blazing with fire to slay a beautiful brown-limbed goddess utterly. It was to be nothing like that.

> With such glad dreams I sought his holy place
> and now with wandering eyes and heart I stand
> Before this supreme mystery of Love:
> Some kneeling girl with passionless pale face,
> An angel with a lily in his hand
> And over both the white wings of a dove.

Mary's sinless womb was Jesus' Eden, his Paradise Garden, which, when her time came, he was forced to leave for a world of sin and death in order to save it.

To show how necessary Mary was, G.K. Chesterton told a symbolic story of a group of Christians who possessed a statue of Mary with the child in her arms. They wanted to get rid of Mary but, if they did, Jesus would have been left up in the air. They, therefore, felt they had no choice but to get rid of both.

Think of the praise of Mary in this book as did Thomas Merton, author and Trappist monk, when he wrote to a fellow poet: 'The great tragedy is that we feel so keenly that love has been twisted out of shape in us and beaten down and crippled. But Christ loves in us, and the compassion of Our Lady keeps her prayer burning like a lamp in the depths of our being. That lamp does not waver. It is the light of the Holy Spirit, invisible, kept alight by her love for us.'

Before Merton, Newman wrote: 'Mary is the most beautiful

flower that ever was seen in the spiritual world. It is the power of God's grace that from this barren and desolate earth there have ever sprung up at all flowers of holiness and glory. And Mary is the Queen of them. She is the Queen of spiritual flowers; and therefore she is called the 'Rose', for the rose is fitly called of all flowers the most beautiful.'

The medieval mystic, Hildegard of Bingen (1098-1179), was one of the most remarkable women in the history of the church, abbess, philosopher, teacher, theologian, botanist, medical scientist, painter, poet, composer, visionary, adviser of popes and kings.

She often saw visions of Mary. Sometimes she was the womanly Wisdom, shaped and shining like a sapphire, which was with God before the world was made. Sometimes she appeared as *Ecclesia*, the church, the Bride of Christ more dazzling than the Bride of the *Song of Songs*, a giant icon dwarfing the world.

Perhaps because Midnight Mass is called *Missa Prima Galli Cantu*, The First Mass of Cock Crow, Hildegard loved to be first up in the morning to hear cockcrow. In the ensuing *Magnum Silentium*, the Great Silence of the new-born world, Mary helped her compose the antiphons of the Mass by singing in her inner ear.

O *Ecclesia*, your eyes are like sapphires,
Your ears are like the mount of Bethel.
You have opened for us
The barred Gate of eternity.

Mary the Virgin's flower
Spreads everywhere, lit by the pinky dawn,
Your nose is a column of incense and myrrh
Your mouth is the sound of many waters.

Hildegard spoke of God green-fingered like a gardener,
and she heard him say to her:

I am the breeze that nurtures all things green.
I encourage blossoms to flourish with ripening fruits.

I am the rain coming from the dew
that causes the grasses to laugh
with the joy of life.

Hildegard saw Mary as the 'One Who Has Greened The
World'. She has moistened the world's dryness, making it
fruitful again. Mary is herself a green tree in which all the
birds of the air find a nest.

Your womb held the world's joy
When heaven's harmony
Chimed out of you like a bell,
Because, holy Virgin, within you
You bore the Christ who made
Your chasteness glow in God.
Like thick dew that livens
And greens the grass.
You, too, are an ever alive-green,
O Mother of all delight.

In her poem, *O Viridissima Virga,* Hildegard greets Mary as
'The Greenest Stem':

Hail, greenest stem
which in the gusting wind of the prayers
of the saints was brought forth.
Since the time has come
when you flourished amongst your friends,
hail, hail to you,
because the warmth of the sun keeps you moist
like the scent of balsam.
For the fairest flower has blossomed in you
and perfumed all scents
which had been parched.
And these all appeared in fullest greenness.

Long before Merton or Newman or Dante, four centuries before even Hildegard, St Lomman, a 7th century Irish abbot from Trim in County Meath, spoke 'The Praises of Mary', with their chorus, 'Mary, Loving Mary, Our joy and our delight.'

These praises, passed on orally, were only written down in the 20th century. Down the ages, these praises were developed like folk songs.

Joy of the Father,
Love of the Son,
Delight of the Holy Spirit,
Delight of the Most High God.
Thou who knew not man,
Mother of the Holy One,
Mother of him who was never made.
He drank life from thy breasts.
Before Adam he knew thee,

To Adam he told of thee.
Angels and saints feast on thy beauty.
Delight of God,
Peerless Mary,
Thy face is heavenly beauty.
Straight Way without spot,
Beautiful flower of every perfume,
Heavenly rose, whose beauty draws all.
Choicest and rarest flower of the Father's garden;
Tended by his angels.
Gentle Mary, loving Mary.

Heavenly wind,
Spring rain,
Blinding Light that overcasts the sun.
Mightier than the mountains.
Greater than the seas.
The sun is thy chariot,
The moon and stars thy playthings
The clouds skip like lambs around thy feet.
Beauty that captivates all hearts.
Light that dispels all darkness,
Mary, whiter than the snows.

At thy consent angels sang hymns of great joy.
The Father Eternal smiled on thee.
The Son became thine own.
The Divine Spirit took thee unto himself
Silent Mary, the Holy Spirit spoke through thee.

All men claim thee.
All peoples bless thy name.

Broken-hearted Mary at the cross.
You saw the rabble mock thy Son.
You saw the lance open his side.
You saw them cast dice for his garments.
You who care for all,
could not give him to drink, when he cried, I thirst.
He gave thee to us as our mother.
You saw him die.

Crimson rose of heavenly fragrance.
From thy pure flesh was made food for us
who know thy Son.
Beautiful Mary, you raised women to a new dignity.
Thy body did not know corruption.
Peaceful sleep fell upon thee.
Thy feet rested on the wings of angels.
In their hands they carried thee.
The heavens opened to thee.
You reign with thy Son.

You come, not as the triumphant warrior
in terrible array ,
But as the gentle mother calling,
calling thy children to thee.

Dove of God, thy voice is sweeter
than the thrush and the lark.
Angels stay their journey to hear thee.
Your words are sweeter than honey.
Your eyes are beautiful and gentle,
We have no fear of thee.

You hear the cry of your children;
You, their mother, will hasten to help.
You gladden the hearts that mourn.
You dry the eyes that weep.
Mother of the widow and orphan.
Safe home to the outcast.
Thy smile is peace.
O Mary, our Mother, lead us home.
O Mary, when our eyes close in our last sleep,
and open to behold thy Son, the just judge,
and the angel opens the book,
and the enemy accuses us,
in that terrible hour, come to our aid,
be with us.

When death came to Joseph,
you and your Son were with him,
Thy Son to judge, thou to console.
O happy Joseph!
When death comes for us, be near us.

O Mary, we are thy children,
Thou art our mother.
As little children we come to thee,
knowing no fear.
O Mary, he changed water into wine for thee,
even as he said: My hour has not yet come.

Now he would not refuse thee,
when you plead for us thy children.

There shall be neither night nor day to thy praises.
Adoration to the Father who created thee!
Adoration to the Son who took flesh from thee!
Adoration to the Holy Spirit, thy Divine Spouse!
Three in One, One in Three.
Equal in all things.
To him be glory for ever and for ever. Amen.

The Irish looked on Jesus as:

The Virgin's nurseling,
Child of the white-footed,
Deathless, inviolate,
Bright-bodied Maiden.

Together with the Spaniards, the Portuguese, the Italians and the French, the Irish spread their love for this Maiden across the Old World and the New so that now not only Europe but North and South America, Australia and New Zealand are full of Catholics repeating daily:

Blessed art thou among women,
and blessed is the fruit of thy womb, Jesus.

2. Favourite Prayers to Mary

Prayer is the life of the soul and the church's favourite prayer to Mary is the *Ave Maria*:

Hail Mary, full of grace,

the Lord is with thee.

Blessed art thou amongst women

and blessed is the fruit of thy womb Jesus.

Holy Mary, Mother of God,

pray for us sinners,

now and at the hour of our death. Amen.

The next favourite is the old version of Mary's own prayer the *Magnificat* when her heart was like a wineskin ready to burst:

My soul doth magnify the Lord

And my spirit hath rejoiced in God my Saviour

Because he hath regarded the lowliness of his handmaid,

For behold, from henceforth all generations shall call me
blessed

for he who is mighty hath done great things to me

and holy is his name

and his mercy is from generation to generation

to those who fear him.

He hath shown might in his arm,

he hath scattered the proud in the conceit of their hearts,

He hath put down the mighty from their thrones

And exalted the lowly,

He hath filled the hungry with good things,
And the rich he hath sent empty away.
He hath remembered Israel his servant,
As he spoke to our fathers,
To Abraham and his seed for ever.

The oldest prayer to the Virgin, found in a Greek papyrus, c.300, is known as *Sub Tuum Praesidium*, Under Thy Protection:

We turn to you for protection,
holy Mother of God.
Listen to our prayers
and help us in our needs.
Save us from every danger,
glorious and blessed Virgin.

The 16th century prayer, *Memorare*, Remember, was once attributed to St Bernard:

Remember, O most gracious Virgin Mary,
that never was it known
that anyone who fled to thy protection,
implored thy help or sought thy intercession
was left unaided.
Inspired by this confidence,
we fly unto thee, O Virgin of virgins our Mother.
To thee do we come,
before thee we stand,
sinful and sorrowful.
O Mother of the Word Incarnate,
despise not our petitions,
but in thy mercy, hear and answer us. Amen.

Few prayers are as popular as the 6th century *Hail Holy Queen*:

Hail, holy Queen,
Mother of Mercy,
Hail our life, our sweetness and our hope.
To thee do we cry, poor banished children of Eve,
To thee do we send up our sighs,
mourning and weeping in this vale of tears.
Turn, then, O most gracious advocate,
Thine eyes of mercy towards us.
And after this our exile,
Show unto us the fruit of thy womb, Jesus,
O clement, O loving, O sweet Virgin Mary.

Since the *Salve Regina* is often sung in Latin, here it is in the original:

Salve Regina, Mater misericordiae:
Vita dulcedo, et spes nostra, salve.
Ad te clamamus, exsules, filii Hevae.
Ad te suspiramus, gementes
et flentes in hac lacrimarum valle.
Eia ergo, Advocata nostra,
illos tuos misericordes oculos ad nos converte.
Et Jesum, benedictum fructum ventris tui,
nobis post hoc exsilium ostende.
O clemens: O pia: O dulcis Virgo Maria.

Jean Francois Millet's much loved 1859 painting of the Angelus shows two peasants, a man and a woman, pausing from their labours to pray. Their heads are bowed. His field fork is stuck in the ground beside him, her basket with potatoes in lies at her feet. On the horizon is the spire of a village church from which comes the peal of the Angelus bells. The Madonna is giving a working man and woman a short break of peace and rest in a day of heavy toil.

The angel of the Lord declared unto Mary.

And she conceived of the Holy Ghost.

Hail Mary …

Behold the handmaid of the Lord.

Be it done unto me according to Thy word.

Hail Mary …

And the Word was made flesh.

And dwelt among us.

Hail Mary …

Pray for us, O holy Mother of God.

That we may be made worthy of the promises of Christ.

Let us pray

Pour forth, we beseech Thee, O Lord, Thy grace into our hearts, that we to whom the Incarnation of Christ, Thy Son, was made known by the message of an angel, may by his passion and cross be brought to the glory of his resurrection. Through the same Christ our Lord. Amen.

On the 80th anniversary of 13 October 1917, when the 'dance of the sun' occurred, Pope John Paul II turned in spirit to the shrine of Fatima. 'Dear pilgrims,' he said, 'as though wanting to embrace all humanity, I ask you to say in her name and for her sake this prayer:

We fly to thy patronage, O holy Mother of God.

Despise not our petitions in our necessities,

but deliver us from all dangers,
O glorious and blessed Virgin.

Another ancient prayer is the *Regina Coeli* by St Athanasius:
Queen of Heaven, rejoice, alleluia,
For he whom thou wast worthy to bear, alleluia,
Has risen, as he said, alleluia,
Pray for us to our God, alleluia.

Rejoice and be glad, O Virgin Mary, alleluia,
For the Lord is risen indeed, alleluia.

God our Father, thou hast given joy to the world through
the resurrection of thy Son, our Lord Jesus Christ.
Through the prayers of his Mother, the Virgin Mary,
bring us to the happiness of eternal life. We ask this
through our Lord, Jesus Christ.

St Francis wrote these *Praises of the Blessed Virgin:*
Hail God's Palace;
Hail his Tabernacle;
Hail his Home.
Hail his Vestment;
Hail his Handmaid;
Hail his Mother
And hail all you holy virtues,
which through the grace and illumination
of the Holy Spirit
are infused into the hearts of the faithful,
so that from those unfaithful
you make them faithful to God.

The most popular of Marian sites is Guadalupe where this prayer is said:

Our Lady of Guadalupe,
Mystical Rose,
intercede for the holy church,
protect the Holy Father,
help all who invoke you in their needs.
Since you are the ever Virgin Mary
and Mother of the true God,
obtain for us from Jesus, your most holy Son
the grace of a firm faith,
sweet hope amid the bitterness of life,
a burning charity
and the precious gift of final perseverance.
Our Lady of Guadalupe, Patroness of the Americas,
pray for us.
Mystical Rose, pray for us.

In the dioceses of the United States, Our Lady of Guadalupe is celebrated on December 12. Here is the opening prayer of the memorial of Our Lady of Guadalupe:

God of power and mercy,
you blessed the Americas at Tepeyac
with the presence of the Virgin Mary of Guadalupe.
May her prayers help all men and women
to accept each other as brothers and sisters.
Through your justice present in our hearts
may your peace reign in the world.
We ask this through our Lord Jesus Christ, your Son,
who lives and reigns with you and the Holy Spirit,
one God, for ever and ever. Amen.

From among the short or aspirational prayers to Mary, we begin with the prayer on the Miraculous Medal:

O Mary conceived without sin,

pray for us who have recourse to thee.

Holy Mary, pray for us.

Immaculate heart of Mary,

Pray for us now and at the hour of our death.

Sweet heart of Mary, be my salvation.

Our Lady, Queen of peace, pray for us.

From the beginnings of the faith in Scotland, Mary was held in such esteem, Jesus was usually referred to as Son of Mary. Here is a Scots' Gaelic prayer full of what someone called the rainbow-light of poetry:

In my deeds,

In my words,

In my wishes,

In my reason,

And in the fulfilling of my desires,

In my sleep,

In my dreams,

In my repose,

In my thoughts,

In my heart and soul always,

May the blessed Virgin Mary,

And the promised Branch of Glory dwell,

Oh! in my heart and soul always,

May the blessed Virgin Mary,

And the fragrant Branch of Glory dwell.

Barra fishermen were helped to brave the high seas around the Western Isles by singing this hymn:

Our Mother,
Holy Mary Mother,
has her arm under our head.
Our pillow is the arm of Mary,
Mary the Holy Mother.

Here are a few Scots Celtic aspirations:

Jesu, thou Son of Mary
Have mercy upon us.
Jesu, thou Son of Mary.
Make peace with us.

Oh with us be and for us be
Where we shall longest be.
Be about the morning of our course
Be about the closing of our life.

I bathe my face
In the nine rays of the sun
As Mary bathed her Son
In rich fermented milk.

Honey be in my mouth
Affection be in my face.
The love that Mary gave her Son
Be in the heart of all flesh for me.

I am lying down tonight,
With Mary and her Son,
With the Mother of my King
Who is shielding me from harm.

I will not lie me down with evil,
Nor shall evil lie down with me,
But I will lie down with my God
And my God lie down with me.

Finally, a modern prayer in honour of the Virgin, 'Mary of
the Starlight':

May Mary – honoured in so many places
in great cathedrals and in lowly grass –
may she bless you and keep you.
May the Morning Star shine gently on your face
and the Evening Star show you your way home.
May the Star of the Sea guide you
across life's stormy waters
till you find safe harbour
and peace for your souls at the last.

3. Favourite Hymns to Mary

Africans have a proverb, 'Take the song from someone's heart and he dies.'

No prayers give greater pleasure
than hymns and carols sung together.

Hildegard of Bingen heard music singing through her while exuding the fragrance of flowers. Praising God in music, she said, is essential to each soul as it was for King David. The Mass that was only 'said', that was without music, seemed to be lacking in some way. The flute and other instruments are God's voice and his compassion; and song is a 'swaying bridge between heaven and earth'.

All Christians have their favourite hymns to Our Lady. We can print a small selection from the host available. Apologies if you cannot find your favourites here.

The first is Monsignor Ronald Knox's translation of Dante's lines from the *Paradiso* on the Virgin Mother:

Maiden, yet a Mother,
Daughter of thy Son,
High beyond all other –
Lowlier is none;
Thou the consummation
Planned by God's decree,
When our lost creation
Nobler rose in thee.

Thus his place preparéd,
He who all things made
'Mid his creatures tarried,
In thy bosom laid;

There his love he nourished, -
Warmth that gave increase
To the Root whence flourished
Our eternal peace.

Noon on Sion's mountain
Is thy charity;
Hope its living fountain
Finds, on earth, in thee;
Lady, such thy power,
He, who grace would buy
Not as of thy dower,
Without wings would fly.

Nor alone thou hearest
When thy name we hail;
Often thou art nearest
When our voices fail;
Mirrored in thy fashion
All creation's good,
Mercy, might, compassion
Grace thy womanhood.

Lady, lest our vision,
Striving heavenward, fail,
Still let thy petition
With thy son prevail,

Unto whom all merit,
Power and majesty,
With the Holy Spirit
And the Father be.

F. W. Weatherell wrote the next hymn:

Mary Immaculate, star of the morning,
Chosen before the creation began,
Chosen to bring for thy bridal adorning,
Woe to the serpent and rescue to man.

Here, in an orbit of shadow and sadness,
Veiling thy splendour, thy course thou hast run;
Now that art throned in all glory and gladness,
Crowned by the hand of thy Saviour and Son.

Sinners, we worship thy sinless perfection;
Fallen and weak for thy pity we plead;
Grant us the shield of thy sovereign protection,
Measure thine aid by the depth of our need.

Frail is our nature, and strict our probation,
Watchful the foe that would lure us to wrong;
Succour our souls in the hour of temptation,
Mary Immaculate, tender and strong.

See how the wiles of the serpent assail us,
See how we waver and flinch in the flight;
Let thine immaculate merit avail us,
Make of our weakness a proof of thy might.

Bend from thy throne at the voice of our crying,
Bend to the earth which thy footsteps have trod;

Stretch out thine arms to us living and dying,
Mary immaculate, Mother of God.

Ave Maris Stella was written by an unknown author before
the 9th century.

Hail thou star of ocean
Portal of the sky
Ever virgin mother
Of the Lord Most High

O! by Gabriel's Ave,
Uttered long ago,
Eva's name reversing
Established peace below

Break the captives' fetters,
Light on blindness pour,
All our ills expelling,
Every bliss implore

As thou art our Mother,
Offer him our sighs,
Who for us incarnate
Did not thee despise

Virgin of all virgins
To thy shelter take us,
Gentlest of the gentle
Chaste and gentle make us.

Still, as on we journey,
Help our weak endeavour,
Till with thee and Jesus
We rejoice forever

Through the highest heaven,
To the Almighty Three
Father, Son and Spirit,
One same glory be. Amen.

St Alphonsus, author of *The Glories of Mary*, wrote *O Mother Blest*, now an established favourite:

O Mother blest, whom God bestows
On sinners and on just,
What joy, what hope thou givest those
Who in thy mercy trust.
Thou art clement, thou art chaste,
Mary, thou art fair;
Of all mothers sweetest, best;
None with thee compare.

O heavenly Mother, mistress sweet!
It never yet was told
That suppliant sinner left thy feet
Unpitied, unconsoled.
Thou art clement, etc.

O Mother pitiful and mild,
Cease not to pray for me;
For I do love thee as a child,
And sigh for love of thee.
Thou art clement, etc.

Most powerful Mother, all men know
Thy Son denies thee nought;
Thou askest, wishes it, and lo!
His power thy will hath wrought.
Thou art clement, etc.

O Mother blest, for me obtain,
Ungrateful though I be,
To love that God who first could deign
To show such love for me.
Thou art clement, thou art chaste,
Mary, thou art fair;
Of all mothers sweetest, best;
None with thee compare.

One of the most popular of all Marian hymns is *Hail,
Queen of Heaven* by John Lingard:

Hail, Queen of heav'n, the ocean star,
Guide of the wand'rer here below:
Thrown on life's surge, we claim thy care –
Save us from peril and from woe.
Mother of Christ, star of the sea,
Pray for the wanderer, pray for me.

O gentle, chaste and spotless Maid,
We sinners make our prayers through thee;
Remind thy Son that he has paid
The price of our iniquity.
Virgin most pure, star of the sea,
Pray for the sinner, pray for me.

Sojourners in this vale of tears,
To thee, blest advocate, we cry;
Pity our sorrows, calm our fears,
And soothe with hope our misery.
Refuge in grief, star of the sea,
Pray for the mourner, pray for me.

And while to him who reigns above,
In Godhead One, in Persons Three,
The source of life, of grace, of love,
Homage we pay on bended knee;
Do thou, bright Queen, star of the sea,
Pray for thy children, pray for me.

An 18th century hymn, *O Sanctissima*, is sung most often in
its original Latin:

O sanctissima, O piissima,
Dulcis virgo Maria!
Mater amata, intemerata,
Ora, Ora, ora pro nobis.

Tu solatium et refugium,
Virgo mater Maria!
Quidquid optamus, per te speramus,
Ora, Ora, ora pro nobis.

The next hymn is *Sing of Mary, Pure and Lowly:*

Sing of Mary, pure and lowly,
Virgin mother undefiled,
Sing of God's own Son most holy,
Who became her little child.

Fairest child of fairest mother,
God the Lord who came to earth,
Word made flesh, our very brother,
Takes our nature by his birth.

Sing of Jesus, Son of Mary,
In the home at Nazareth.
Toil and labour cannot weary
Love enduring unto death.
Constant was the love he gave her,
Though he went forth from her side,
Forth to preach, and heal, and suffer,
Till on Calvary he died.

Glory be to God the Father;
Glory be to God the Son;
Glory be to God the Spirit;
Glory to the Three in One.
From the heart of blessed Mary,
From all saints the song ascends,
And the church the strain re-echoes
Unto earth's remotest ends.

The *Stabat Mater*, a meditation on Mary's sorrows at the foot of the cross, dates from the 14th century.

At the cross her station keeping
Stood the mournful mother weeping,
Close to Jesus to the last.
Through her heart, his sorrow sharing,
All his bitter anguish bearing,
Lo! the piercing sword had passed.

O how sad and sore distressed
Was that mother, highly blessed,
Of the Sole-Begotten One.
Mournful, with heart's prostration,
Mother meek, the bitter passion
Saw she of her glorious Son.

Who on Christ's dear mother gazing,
In her trouble so amazing,
Born of woman, would not weep?
Who on Christ's dear mother thinking,
Such a cup of sorrow drinking,
Would not share her sorrow deep?

For his people's sins rejected,
Saw her Jesus unprotected.
Saw with thorns, with scourges rent.
Saw her Son from judgement taken,
Her Beloved in death forsaken,
Till his Spirit forth he sent.

Fount of love and holy sorrow,
Mother, may my spirit borrow
Somewhat of your woe profound.
Unto Christ with pure emotion,
Raise my contrite heart's devotion,
To read love in every wound.

Those five wounds on Jesus smitten,
Mother! in my heart be written,
Deep as in your own they be.
You, your Saviour's cross did bare,

You, your Son's rebuke did share.
Let me share them both with thee.

In the passion of my Maker,
Be my sinful soul partaker,
Weep 'til death and weep with you.
Mine with you be that sad station,
There to watch the great salvation,
Wrought upon the atoning tree.

Virgin, you of virgins fairest,
May the bitter woe thou bearest
Make on me impression deep.
Thus Christ's dying may I carry,
With him in his passion tarry,
And his wounds in memory keep.

Jesus, may your cross defend me,
And your mother's prayer befriend me;
Let me die in your embrace.
When to dust my dust returns,
Grant a soul, that to you yearns,
In your paradise a place. Amen.

Frederick Faber's hymn, *Mother of Mercy*, said Cardinal Newman, was his best:

Mother of Mercy, day by day
My love of thee grows more and more;
Thy gifts are strewn upon my way,
Like sands upon the great sea-shore.

Though poverty and work and woe
The masters of my life may be,
When times are worst, who does not know
Darkness is light with love of thee?

But scornful men have coldly said
Thy love was leading me from God;
And yet in this I did but tread
The very path my Saviour trod.

They know but little of thy worth
Who speak these heartless words to me;
For what did Jesus love on earth
One half so tenderly as thee?

Get me the grace to love thee more;
Jesus will give, if thou wilt plead;
And, mother, when life's cares are o'er,
Oh, I shall love thee then indeed.

Jesus, when his three hours were run,
Bequeathed thee from the cross to me;
And oh! how can I love thy Son,
Sweet mother, if I love not thee?

The Assumption by Sir John Beaumont (1583-1727) moves
from Mary's sorrows to her exultation:

Who is she ascends so high,
Next the heavenly King,
Round about whom angels fly
And her praises sing?

Who is she adorned with light,
Makes the sun her robe,
At whose feet the queen of night
Lays her changing globe?

This is she in whose pure womb
Heaven's Prince remainéd;
Therefore in no earthly tomb
Can she be containéd.

Heaven she was, which held that fire,
Whence the world took light,
And to heaven doth now aspire
Flames with flames t'unite.

She that did so clearly shine
When our day begun,
See how bright her beams decline:
Now she sits with the Sun.

Millions of pilgrims will confirm that the words of the
Lourdes Hymn bring back the happy experience of being
in a place where the sick are treated with the respect due to
Christ himself. Up to 60 verses exist. Here is a selection
from them.

The bells of the Angelus
Call us to pray.
In sweet tones announcing
The sacred Ave.
Ave, ave, ave Maria;
Ave, ave, ave Maria.

An angel of mercy
led Bernadette's feet
where flows the deep torrent
Our Lady to greet. *(Chorus)*

She prayed to our mother
that God's will be done.
She prayed for his glory
that his kingdom come. *(Chorus)*

Immaculate Mary
your praises we sing
who reign now with Christ,
our redeemer and king. *(Chorus)*

In heaven the blessed
your glory proclaim.
On earth now your children
invoke your fair name. *(Chorus)*

Immaculate Mary!
Our hearts are on fire.
That title so wondrous
fills all our desire. *(Chorus)*

We pray for God's glory,
may his kingdom come!
We pray for his Vicar,
our Father, and Rome. *(Chorus)*

We pray for our mother
the church upon earth,
and bless, sweetest Lady,
the land of our birth. *(Chorus)*

For poor, sick afflicted
thy mercy we crave
and comfort the dying
thou light of the grave.
Ave, ave, ave Maria;
Ave, ave, ave Maria.

4. Christmas:
The World's Favourite Festival

To enter the grand old Bethlehem church where the first Christmas occurred you must pass through the low Door of Humility. Unless you are already a child, you need to bow your head.

Marking the spot in the grotto where Jesus was born is a fourteen-point silver star set in white marble. An inscription around it reads, *Hic de Virgine Maria Jesus Christus natus est,* Here Jesus Christ was born of the Virgin Mary.

Christmas is the easiest festival to understand. Paul Claudel speaks of Jesus, Mary and Joseph, three poor people who love each other, and it is they who are going to change the world.

Joseph is the almost forgotten figure of the three. Silent, dependable, trusting, willing to believe the unbelievable, he comes across as essentially a good man, a good husband, the man who in Nazareth was called carpenter before Jesus was. In time, he was to teach his trade to his boy, for Jesus was his boy, too, being his wife's child.

Rilke, in his poem 'Joseph's Suspicion', captures the agony Joseph underwent before he saw the light:

Long and carefully the angel spoke
Over this man with fists tight clenched.
'Do you not see in every fold of her
That she is sweet and lovely as God's morning?'

Still the man stared blackly at him,
Muttering, 'What has changed her, then?'
'Oh, Carpenter,' the angel cried,
'Do you not yet see in this the Lord's own hand?

'Because you make boards from wood
Does this entitle you with pride
To queruously lift your voice to him
Who makes in silence buds and leaves
Sprout from that same wood?'

Ah, yes. Yes. He understood. Yes.
He looked up, shaken, to find the angel gone.
Slowly, he removed his cap
And sang his song of praise.

At first, Christians did not celebrate Christmas because no one knew the date of Jesus' birth.

Under the old Julian calendar, the winter solstice took place on 25 December. This turning point of the year was celebrated as the Sun's Birthday when the days begin to lengthen and the weather grows warmer.

In Syria and Egypt, religious groups who worshipped the heavenly virgin or the heavenly goddess retired into a dark shrine emerging at midnight to cry aloud, 'The Virgin has brought forth, the light is waxing.' The Egyptians even brought into view a new-born child, his entry into the world coinciding with the birth of the sun.

For many peoples, this was a time of feasting, gift-giving, and, often, heavy drinking.

Seeing that Christians, too, were attracted to this festival, the Western church decided in the 4th century to celebrate it as Christ's Mass, the birth of Jesus the Son of God from the Virgin Mary.

It was a mixed blessing. A pagan festival was christianised but the feast of Christ's birth became tinged with pagan revelries – what we would call commercialism. But, Christians argued, wasn't Jesus himself given gifts by the shepherds and the Magi?

Christmas turned out to be the best loved festival in the world, adding to the message of the Nativity the lights, the indoor tree, the tinsel, the singing and, of course, the feasting.

What would the world be like now without Christmas? How incalculable would be the loss of the child in the crib and in his mother's arms, of Joseph, the shepherds and the Wise Men from the East and all the carols that celebrate these wonderful events? Certainly, wherever Christmas has been banned, people have always clamoured for its return.

In the old Soviet Union, Christmas was banned with all other religious holidays and replaced with New Year. Citizens bought New Year's trees, gave New Year's presents, sent New Year's cards and drank far too much at New Year's Eve parties. Saint Nicholas was replaced with Grandfather Frost, who was usually accompanied by a snowmaiden. Ironically, it was on a Christmas day that the red flag was lowered over the Kremlin for the last time as Gorbachev resigned as the last Communist leader. Today,

Russia is free to celebrate Christmas and President Putin proclaims himself a believer.

In 1970, the Communist government of Cuba followed the Soviet Union and banned Christmas to allow comrades to take part in the sugar harvest.

In 1997, to prepare for the visit by John Paul II, Christmas was celebrated for the first time in thirty years. Church bells rang out and more than a thousand people packed Havana's cathedral for midnight Mass. Very slowly, Christmas with its spirit of love and peace, is returning to the island.

John Knox, disciple of Calvin was the first to put an end to Christmas in Scotland.

A century later, parliament banned it in England. Oliver Cromwell, Lord Protector, declared Christmas 'an extreme forgetfulness of Christ, by giving liberty to carnal and sensual delights'. However, when many town criers shouted 'No Christmas! No Christmas!' the people rioted. Ten thousand gathered in Canterbury, protesting that 'if they could not have Christmas Day, they would have the King back on his throne again'. When King Charles II came to the throne in 1660, he restored Christmas Day.

In the first century of colonial rule, American Puritans frowned on all public Christmas festivities. They associated them with English dicing, drunkenness and wild behaviour, as well as with incense, monkish jargon and episcopacy. Christmas was, after all, the Romish word for Christ's Mass.

December 25th was a normal work day and all the shops were kept open. Any person who observed it as a holiday was fined five shillings, quite a sum in those days. As late as 1847, no college in New England had Christmas vacations.

Queen Victoria's consort, Prince Albert, introduced the German custom of the Christmas tree into England. Before then the chief decoration was the 'kissing bough', two hoops made into a circle and decorated with greenery, oranges, apples and mistletoe.

From England, the Christmas tree spread to America. The first in the White House was in 1856. By 1958 Mamie Eisenhower had twenty-seven of them in the White House.

It was, however, Charles Dickens, known as the Santa Claus of English literature, who most changed the American Christmas. On 9 June, 1870, a Cockney barrow-girl famously reacted to the day's most important news with 'Dickens dead? Then will Father Christmas die too?'

Dickens was the first to join 'Merry' and 'Christmas' in the greeting 'Merry Christmas' in *A Christmas Carol* (1843). Ebenezer Scrooge hated the phrase. 'If I had my will,' he groaned, 'every idiot who goes about with "Merry Christmas" on his lips should be boiled with his own pudding, and buried with a stake of holly through his heart.'

Though Dickens never mentioned Christ and celebrated the religion of the hearth not the altar, the spirit of *A Christmas Carol* is the religion of the heart. Scrooge's nephew describes it 'as a good time; a kind, forgiving, char-

itable, pleasant time; the only time I know of, in the long
calendar of the year, when men and women seem by one
consent to open their shut-up hearts freely, and to think of
people below them as if they really were fellow-travellers
to the grave, and not another race of creatures bound on
other journeys. And therefore, uncle, though it has never
put a scrap of gold or silver in my pocket, I believe that it
has done me good, and will do me good; and I say, God
bless it!'

The New England Puritans were not unlike Scrooge with
his 'Bah! Humbug!' It took the genius of Dickens to bring
the old English love of Christmas to New England.

By the time American novelist, Willa Cather (1873-1947)
wrote for the *Nebraska State Journal*, Christmas was well
established. She describes an African-American church in
which the congregation were singing *Peace on Earth*.
Afterwards, an old grey-haired Negro in a frock coat and
wearing two pairs of glasses stood up and read the old, old
story of shepherds and the babe born in Bethlehem. He
became very excited and his voice trembled.

'When he finished,' said Cather, 'he looked up at the ceil-
ing with eager misty eyes as though he could see the light
of the heavenly messenger shining in upon him. It is a
beautiful story, this, of the holiest and purest childhood on
earth, beautiful even to those who cannot understand it, as
dreams are sweet to men without hope.'

Hispanics now make up 12 per cent of the US population.
On present trends, 47 per cent of future US growth will be

among Hispanics. In recent years, there have been 33 million immigrants to the USA from Latin America, two thirds of them Mexican. They brought their own devotions with them, especially at Christmas time.

Firstly, they set up altars in the home. The domestic altar is a kind of visible history of a family and a faith that has endured over the generations.

The tradition goes back to pre-Christian times. Providentially, Catholics found this practice indispensable when Mexico got its independence from Spain. With a crackdown by the state, and priests in short supply, without the home altars preserved by the mother or female prayer leader – the *rezadora* – the faith might not have endured.

Today, Latinos put on their altars candles and flowers. But they add photos of their loved ones, living and dead, together with crucifixes and pictures of Our Lady such as the Virgin of Guadalupe or the Virgin of Charity of Cobre, patroness of Cuba. The altar is the focus of prayers, the most popular being the rosary. The favourite feast is, of course, the *nacimiento* or Nativity when the altar becomes a stable in which the Christ-Child is born of the Virgin Mary.

This mingling of the secular and sacred provides a kind of sacred space in which each family welcomes strangers as if they were Jesus and Mary. This is what lies behind the popular phrase, *Mi casa es su casa,* My home is your home. They will not turn away the Holy Family as once they were turned away from the inn in Bethlehem.

The United States is justly proud of its separation of church and state, but it has brought with it certain problems over Christmas. While American families are free to celebrate Christmas in their millions, the US government is no more authorised than Cuba or the old Soviet Union to celebrate it officially or teach it in schools.

In 1953, President Eisenhower sent out 1,100 official White House Christmas cards. George W. Bush sends a million, though he is careful to speak of the 'Greetings of the Season' and not to show a Christmas crib. No President wants to upset Jews or Muslims. Which is why J. F. K. felt free at Christmas to quote Charles Dickens but not Jesus Christ.

Ronald Reagan went his own way. He complained once that US coins bear the words 'In God We Trust' and that he took the oath of office asking God's help. When Americans pledge allegiance to the flag, he said, we proclaim we are a nation under God but we can't mention his name in a public school or even sing non-denominational religious hymns. As to Christmas, it can be celebrated in schools with pine trees, tinsel and reindeers. 'But there must be no mention of the man whose birthday is being celebrated. One wonders how a teacher would answer if a student asked why it was called Christmas.'

He silenced criticism by saying that the Nativity story is known by all faiths as a hymn to the brotherhood of man. Its spirit is present when those of every creed bring love and understanding to the hearts of their fellow man.

On 20 December, 1983, he said in a radio address: 'Of all the songs ever sung at Christmastime, the most wonderful of all was the song of exaltation heard by the shepherds while tending their flocks on the night of Christ's birth.'

Four days later, a young girl, Amy Benham, helped him light the national tree. In President Reagan's words:

> Amy had said that the tree that lights up our country must be seen all the way to heaven. And she said that her wish was to help me turn on its lights. Well, Amy's wish came true. But the greatest gift was mine, because I saw her eyes light up with hope and joy just as brightly as the lights on our national tree. And I'm sure they were both seen all the way to heaven, and they made the angels sing.

> Christmas is a time for children, and rightly so. We celebrate the birthday of the Prince of Peace who came as a babe in a manger. Some celebrate Christmas as the birthday of a great teacher and philosopher. But to other millions of us, Jesus is much more. He is divine, living assurance that God so loved the world he gave us his only begotten Son so that by believing in him and learning to love each other we could one day be together in paradise. It's been said that all the kings who ever reigned, that all the parliaments that ever sat have not done as much to advance the cause of peace on earth and goodwill to men as the man from Galilee.

In 1986, Reagan sent a Christmas message from the American people to Christians in the Soviet Union, joining them as one family under God the Father:

Of the many apparent paths to peace, we have seen one path that does lead to peace, the same path illuminated by Jesus Christ – the path of truth and love and humility. The date that you and we celebrate Christmas may be different. But the meaning and magnificence of what we celebrate – the divine birth of one man, hero, strong yet tender, Prince of Peace – is the same. This birth brought forth good tidings of great joy to all people. For unto us was born this day a Saviour who is Christ the Lord.

Finally, it has to be said that religion is far too serious not to laugh about it sometimes.

Author Gervase Phinn was once a schools' inspector. He tells of a nativity play he once saw in Glasgow that brought tears to his eyes. It makes the point of Christmas better than any preacher.

The Virgin Mary, in the person of a tiny Glaswegian, was on stage in traditional blue when a sturdily built little fellow, a classmate of hers, stomps on. This is the Archangel Gabriel, aged six, no front teeth, runny nose, draped in a sheet with a bit of tinsel round the bottom.

'Are you all right Mary?' says the angel.

'Aye I'm all right, who are you?'

'I'm the Archangel Gabriel,' he says, 'I've come down to tell you something.'

Mary says, 'Och aye, what you got to tell me, then?'

He says, 'You're having a baby.'

She says, 'I'm having no baby.'

He says, 'You are, God's told me to tell you and you've got to call it Jesus.'

Mary says, 'I like Dougal meself.'

He says, 'No, no, you've got to call it Jesus otherwise you don't get it.'

On comes Joseph with a piece of wood in his hand.

'Are you all right Joseph?' Mary says.

'I'm all right Mary, just a wee bit tired.'

'You sit down,' she says, 'and I'll get you a cup of tea.'

'Fine by me.'

Then she sidles up to him and says, 'Aye Joseph, I've got something to tell you.'

He says, 'Och aye, Mary, what have you got to tell me?'

She says, 'I'm having a baby – and it's not yours.'

5. Favourite Christmas Carols

Once In Royal David's City never ceases echoing in our memories of childhood.

Once in royal David's city
Stood a lowly cattle shed,
Where a mother laid her Baby
In a manger for his bed:
Mary was that mother mild,
Jesus Christ her little child.

He came down to earth from heaven,
Who is God and Lord of all,
And his shelter was a stable,
And his cradle was a stall;
With the poor, and mean, and lowly,
Lived on earth our Saviour holy.

And through all his wondrous childhood
He would honour and obey,
Love and watch the lowly maiden,
In whose gentle arms he lay:
Christian children all must be
Mild, obedient, good as he.

Jesus is our childhood's pattern;
Day by day, like us he grew;
He was little, weak and helpless,
Tears and smiles like us he knew;

And he feeleth for our sadness,
And he shareth in our gladness.

And our eyes at last shall see him,
Through his own redeeming love;
For that child so dear and gentle
Is our Lord in heaven above,
And he leads his children on
To the place where he is gone.

Not in that poor lowly stable,
With the oxen standing by,
We shall see him; but in heaven,
Set at God's right hand on high;
Where like stars his children crowned
All in white shall wait around.

The carol *Sleep, Holy Babe* by H. Caswall (1814-78) is always popular:

Sleep, holy Babe,
Upon thy mother's breast;
Great Lord of earth and sea and sky,
How sweet it is to see thee lie
In such a place of rest.

Sleep, holy Babe,
Thine angels watch around,
All bending low, with folded wings,
Before th'incarnate King of kings,
In reverent awe profound.

Sleep, holy Babe,
While I with Mary gaze
In joy upon that face awhile
Upon the loving infant smile,
Which there divinely plays.

Sleep, holy Babe,
Ah, take thy brief repose:
Too quickly will thy slumbers break
And thou to lengthen'd pains awake,
That death alone shall close.

O Lady blest,
Sweet Virgin, hear my cry;
Forgive the wrong that I have done
To thee, in causing the dear Son
Upon the cross to die.

In 1872, Christina Rossetti wrote *A Christmas Carol:*
In the bleak midwinter, frosty wind made moan,
Earth stood hard as iron, water like a stone;
Snow had fallen, snow on snow, snow on snow,
In the bleak midwinter, long ago.

Our God, heaven cannot hold him, nor earth sustain;
Heaven and earth shall flee away when he comes to reign.
In the bleak midwinter a stable place sufficed
The Lord God Almighty, Jesus Christ.

Enough for him, whom cherubim, worship night and day,
Breastful of milk, and a mangerful of hay;
Enough for him, whom angels fall before,
The ox and ass and camel which adore.

Angels and archangels may have gathered there,
Cherubim and seraphim thronged the air;
But his mother only, in her maiden bliss,
Worshipped the Beloved with a kiss.

What can I give him, poor as I am?
If I were a shepherd, I would bring a lamb;
If I were a Wise Man, I would do my part;
Yet what I can give him: give my heart.

A carol enjoyed by most children is *Oh, Little Town of Bethlehem:*

O little town of Bethlehem,
How still we see thee lie;
Above thy deep and dreamless sleep
The silent stars go by;
Yet in thy dark streets shineth
The everlasting light.
The hopes and fears of all the years
Are met in thee tonight.

For Christ is born of Mary,
And gathered all above,
While mortals sleep the angels keep
Their watch of wondering love.
O morning stars, together
Proclaim the holy birth!
And praises sing to God the King,
And peace to men on earth!

How silently, how silently
The wondrous gift is given!
So God imparts to human hearts
The blessings of his heaven.
No ear may hear his coming;
But in this world of sin,
Where meek souls will receive him still,
The dear Christ enters in.

O holy Child of Bethlehem,
Descend to us, we pray;
Cast out our sin and enter in,
Be born in us today.
We hear the Christmas angels
The great glad tidings tell,
O come to us, abide with us,
Our Lord Emmanuel!

Perhaps we need reminding that Christmas carols are not sentimental ditties but songs of liberation. The next carol comes from the days of African slavery. It centres on the birth of a Mid-Eastern boy 2,000 years ago.

The Virgin Mary had a baby boy,
The Virgin Mary had a baby boy,
The Virgin Mary had a baby boy,
And they say that his name is Jesus.

Refrain:
He came from the glory,
He came from the glorious kingdom.
He came from the glory,
He came from the glorious kingdom.

Oh yes, believer!
Oh yes, believer!
He came from the glory,
He came from the glorious kingdom.

The angels sang when the baby born,
The angels sang when the baby born,
The angels sang when the baby born,
And proclaimed him the Saviour Jesus.

Refrain

The wise men saw where the baby born,
The wise men saw where the baby born,
The wise men saw where the baby born,
And proclaimed him the Saviour Jesus.

Mary Had A Baby is another Negro spiritual. Its simplicity is in perfect harmony with the gospel story as is the repetition of its sad and haunting last line:

Mary had a baby, oh, Lord,
Mary had a baby, oh my Lord,
Mary had a baby, oh Lord,
People keep a-comin' an' the train done gone.

What did she name him? oh, Lord,
What did she name him? oh my Lord,
What did she name him? oh Lord,
People keep a-comin' an' the train done gone.

She named him Jesus, oh, Lord,
She named him Jesus, oh my Lord,
She named him Jesus, oh Lord,
People keep a-comin' an' the train done gone.

Now where was he born? oh, Lord,
Where was he born? oh my Lord,
Where was he born? oh Lord,
People keep a-comin' an' the train done gone.

Born in a stable, oh, Lord,
Born in a stable, oh my Lord,
Born in a stable, oh Lord,
People keep a-comin' an' the train done gone.

And where did she lay him? oh, Lord,
Where did she lay him? oh my Lord,
Where did she lay him? oh Lord,
People keep a-comin' an' the train done gone.

She laid him in a manger, oh, Lord,
Laid him in a manger, oh my Lord,
Laid him in a manger, oh Lord,
People keep a-comin' an' the train done gone.

Mary had a baby, oh, Lord,
Mary had a baby, oh my Lord,
Mary had a baby, oh Lord,
People keep a-comin' an' the train done gone.

Mary's Boy Child is from the Caribbean:
Mary's boy child Jesus Christ,
was born on Christmas Day.
And man will live for evermore,
because of Christmas Day.

Long time ago in Bethlehem,
so the Holy Bible say,

Mary's boy child Jesus Christ,
was born on Christmas Day.

Hark, now hear the angels sing,
a king was born today,
And man will live for evermore,
because of Christmas Day.
Mary's boy child Jesus Christ,
was born on Christmas Day.

While shepherds watch their flocks by night,
they see a bright new shining star,
they hear a choir sing a song,
the music seemed to come from afar.

Hark, now hear the angels sing,
a king was born today,
And man will live for evermore,
because of Christmas Day.

Oh a moment still worth was a glow,
all the bells rang out
there were tears of joy and laughter,
people shouted 'let everyone know,
there is hope for all to find peace'.

Now Joseph and his wife, Mary,
came to Bethlehem that night,
they found no place to bear her child,
not a single room was in sight.

And then they found a little nook
in a stable all forlorn,

and in a manger cold and dark,
Mary's little boy was born.

Hark, now hear the angels sing,
a king was born today,
And man will live for evermore,
because of Christmas Day.
Mary's boy child Jesus Christ,
was born on Christmas Day.

Oh a moment still worth was a glow,
all the bells rang out
there were tears of joy and laughter,
people shouted 'let everyone know,
there is hope for all to find peace'.
Oh my Lord...

A Polish Lullaby here represents the many European favourites:

Sleeping little Jesus, my treasure, my blessing,
While Mary comforts thee tender caressing.
Lullaby little one, who in loving arms lies
Guarding my darling and stilling thy cries.
When thou awakenest, Jesus, my treasure
Raisins and almonds I have for thy pleasure.
High in the heavens a lovely star sees us,
But like the shining sun, my little Jesus.

What Child Is This? is often sung to the music of *Greensleeves*:

What child is this, who, laid to rest
On Mary's lap, is sleeping?
Whom angels greet with anthems sweet,
While shepherds watch are keeping?
This, this is Christ the King,
Whom shepherds guard and angels sing:
Haste, haste to bring him laud,
The Babe, the Son of Mary!

So bring him incense, gold, and myrrh,
Come peasant king to own him,
The King of kings, salvation brings,
Let loving hearts enthrone him.
Raise, raise the song on high,
The Virgin sings her lullaby:
Joy, joy, for Christ is born,
The Babe, the Son of Mary!

Gentle Mary Laid Her Child by Joseph S. Cook was written in
1919:

Gentle Mary laid her child
Lowly in a manger.
There he lay, the Undefiled,
To the world a stranger.
Such a Babe in such a place,
Can he be the Saviour?
Ask the saved of all the race
Who have found his favour.

Angels sang about his birth,
Wise men sought and found him.

Heaven's star shone brightly forth
Glory all around him.

Shepherds saw the wondrous sight,
Hear the angels singing.
All the plains were lit that night,
All the hills were ringing.

Gentle Mary laid her child
Lowly in a manger.
He is still the Undefiled,
But no more a stranger.

Son of God of humble birth,
Beautiful the story.
Praise his name in all the earth.
Hail! The King of Glory!

The Holly and the Ivy is sung by Christians and non-Christians alike:

The holly and the ivy,
When they are both full grown,
Of all the trees that are in the wood,
The holly bears the crown.

O the rising of the sun,
And the running of the deer,
The playing of the merry organ,
Sweet singing in the choir.

The holly bears a blossom
As white as lily flower;
And Mary bore sweet Jesus Christ
To be our sweet Saviour.

The holly bears a berry
As red as any blood;
And Mary bore sweet Jesus Christ
To do poor sinners good.

The holly bears a prickle
As sharp as any thorn;
And Mary bore sweet Jesus Christ
On Christmas day in the morn.

The holly bears a bark
As bitter as any gall;
And Mary bore sweet Jesus Christ
For to redeem us all.

The holly and the ivy,
When they are both full grown,
Of all the trees that are in the wood,
The holly bears the crown.

Perhaps the first American Christmas carol is the most moving of all. Known as *The Huron Carol* it was written by a Jesuit. Jean de Brébeuf SJ, born in Normandy in 1593, was martyred at the hands of the Iroquois in Canada in 1649.

A visionary, he speaks of seeing 'the Blessed Virgin, as though in an azure cloud, nursing the Child Jesus. And through different parts of the cloud there burst forth rays of gold of a marvellous beauty.'

His carol, *Jesous Ahatonnia* (Jesus is Born), written in the Huron language, was adapted from a 16th century French folk song. Since the Hurons have no M, he substituted the

French dipthong *ou*, so 'Mary' appears as 'Ouarie' (pronounced 'Warie'). The second verse in the original goes:

Aloki ekwatatennonten shekwachiendaen
Iontonk ontatiande ndio sen tsatonnharonnion
Ouarie onnawakueton ndio sen tsatonnharonnion
Iesous ahatonnia.

In the English translation, the New Testament images are beautifully adapted to the minds of the Huron people:

'Twas in the moon of wintertime
When all the birds had fled,
That mighty Gitchi Manitou
Sent angel choirs instead;
Before their light the stars grew dim,
And wond'ring hunters heard the hymn:
Jesus, your King is born,
Jesus is born,
In excelsis gloria.

O, hearken to the angels' word,
Do not decline
To heed the message which you heard:
The Child Divine,
As they proclaim, has come this morn
Of Mary pure. Let us adore.
Jesus is born,
In excelsis gloria.

Within a lodge of broken bark
The tender Babe was found,
A ragged robe of rabbit skin

Enwrapp'd his beauty 'round;
But as the hunter braves drew nigh,
The angel song rang loud and high:
Jesus, your King is born,
Jesus is born,
In excelsis gloria.

The earliest moon of wintertime
Is not so round and fair
As was the ring of glory on
The helpless infant there.
The chiefs from far before him knelt
With gifts of fox and beaver pelt.
Jesus, your King is born,
Jesus is born,
In excelsis gloria.

O children of the forest free,
O sons of Manitou,
The Holy Child of earth and heav'n
Is born today for you.
Come kneel before the radiant boy;
Who brings you beauty, peace and joy.
Jesus, your King is born,
Jesus is born,
In excelsis gloria.

The most popular carol of all, known as 'The Song That Went Around The World' is *Silent Night* with its message of peace. The words *Stille Nacht! Heilige Nacht!* were by Joseph Mohr, a young curate born in Salzburg, Austria. The music was by Franz Gruber. It was first heard at Midnight Mass in 1818. In 1839, a music group, the Rainers performed it for the first time in the New World at the Alexander Hamilton Monument outside Trinity Church in New York.

Silent night, holy night,
All is calm, all is bright
Round yon virgin mother and child.
Holy infant so tender and mild,
Sleep in heavenly peace.
Sleep in heavenly peace.

Silent night, holy night,
Shepherds quake at the sight,
Glories stream from heaven afar,
Heavenly hosts sing alleluia;
Christ the Saviour, is born!
Christ the Saviour, is born!

Silent night, holy night,
Son of God, love's pure light
Radiant beams from thy holy face,
With the dawn of redeeming grace,
Jesus, Lord, at thy birth.
Jesus, Lord, at thy birth.

6. Mary in Modern Catholic Poetry

In *The Life of Mary*, Rainer Maria Rilke conveys the sheer wonder of the Annunciation:

When the angel came, he did not shock her,
It was as if a ray of sun or moon
Had come into the room.
She did not even blink.
But when his youthful face bent near hers,
They looked into one another's eyes,
A look so powerful that the outside world
Suddenly emptied
And the visions of crowds, their deeds and struggles,
All went away, leaving just the two of them,
A girl and an angel in a little place,
Astonishing them both
Before the angel sang his song.

The *Magnificat* was put into verse as the *Canticle of Mary* by a popular English composer Samuel Webbe (1742-1816):

My soul gives glory to the Lord,
In God my saviour I rejoice.
My lowliness he did regard,
Exalting me by his own choice.

From this day all shall call me blest,
For he has done great things for me.
Of all great names his is the best,
For it is holy; strong is he.

His mercy goes to all who fear,
From age to age and to all parts.
His arm of strength to all is near;
He scatters those who have proud hearts.

He casts the mighty from their throne
And raises those of low degree;
He feeds the hungry as his own;
The rich depart in poverty.

He raised his servant, Israel,
Rememb'ring his eternal grace,
As from of old he did foretell
To Abraham and all his race.

O Father, Son, and Spirit blest,
In threefold Name are you adored;
To you be ev'ry prayer addrest,
From age to age the only Lord.

Many midwives have noticed the moment when a mother takes her first new-born into her arms for the first time. It is so different from feeling it in her womb. Now she can see it entirely, its features, its bodily shape, its quiet breathing.

After immense joy comes, a shuddering instant later, a fearful alarm. She senses not only its beauty but its fragility. Life suddenly switches from seeming solid to something like the nest of bubbles that a pond spider builds – one puff of air, one bubble at a time – on an underwater reed.

Such ambivalence of feeling! Will her child be happy, will it suffer pain, will its life be fruitful, will it survive and live long years? In the new mother's arms the tiny bundle, feather-light a moment earlier, grows heavy with all her fears and apprehensions.

Once, people thought that a nightingale sang its sweet sad song because it leaned against a thorn. All mothers feel the same sharp pain when they sing lullabies. Mary, too. Her mood of hope and apprehension at the birth of her Son is expressed in *Mary's Prayer*.

This child I hold,
a few days old,
means more to me than gems or gold.
I stroke his face,
his tiny limbs embrace,
and pray my baby son grows full of grace.

This babe I kiss
fills me with bliss.
How could I have dreamed –
have ever dreamed –
of joy like this?

I hear him cry
at night and I
am anxious lest my baby die.
I'm close to tears
and racked with awful fears
at all the pain he'll suffer down the years.

This babe I kiss
fills me with bliss.
How could I have dreamed –

have ever dreamed –
of joy like this?

This son of mine,
A gift divine,
is like a flask of precious wine.
The flask may break,
the red, red wine escape,
and my life, too, his sudden death would take.

This babe I kiss
fills me with bliss.
How could I have dreamed –
have ever dreamed –
of joy like this?

Yet still I trust,
As mothers must,
though life be brief, a dance of dust.
Dear God above,
the bubbling Fount of Love,
protect my child, this white, soft cooing dove.

May heaven be there
to guard with loving care
my darling, my little darling,
this is my prayer.

Charles G. D. Roberts expressed similar feelings in *When Mary the Mother Kissed the Child*.

When Mary the Mother felt faint hands
Beat at her bosom with life's demands,

And nought to her were the kneeling kings,
The serving star and the half-seen wings.
Then was the little of earth made great,
And the man came back to the God's estate.

Nothing could be gentler than *A Cradle Song* by Irish poet,
Padraic Colum.

O men from the fields,
Come gently within.
Tread softly, softly
O men coming in!

Mavourneen is going
From me and from you,
Where Mary will fold him
With mantle of blue!

From reek of the smoke
And cold of the floor
And the peering of things
Across the half-door.

O men of the fields,
Soft, softly come thro'
Mary puts round him
Her mantle of blue.

Chesterton's poem, *A Christmas Carol*, suggests all the new-
ness and innocence that Christ's birth brings to a jaded
world:

The Christ-child lay on Mary's lap,
His hair was like a light.

(O weary, weary were the world,
But here is all aright.)

The Christ-child lay on Mary's breast
His hair was like a star.
(O stern and cunning are the kings,
But here the true hearts are.)

The Christ-child lay on Mary's heart,
His hair was like a fire.
(O weary, weary is the world,
But here the world's desire.)

The Christ-child stood on Mary's knee,
His hair was like a crown,
And all the flowers looked up at him,
And all the stars looked down.

In the 17th century, Richard Crashaw expresses amazement
at God's humility in coming to earth as a babe:

That the Great Angel-blinding Light should shrink
His blaze, to shine in a poor Shepherd's eye;
That the unmeasur'd God so low should sink,
As Pris'ner in a few poor rags to lie;
That from his mother's breast he milk should drink ...
Welcome all wonders in one sight!
Eternity in a span,
Summer in winter, day in night,
Heaven in earth and God in man;
Great little one! Whose all embracing birth
Lifts earth to heav'n, stoops heav'n to earth.

Perhaps the greatest Marian poem ever written is Gerard Manley Hopkins' *The Blessed Virgin Compared To The Aire We Breathe:*

> This air, which, by life's law,
> My lung must draw and draw
> Now but to breathe its praise,
> Minds me in many ways
> Of her who not only
> Gave God's infinity
> Dwindled to infancy
> Welcome in womb and breast,
> Birth, milk, and all the rest
> But mothers each new grace
> That does now reach our race –
> Mary Immaculate,
> Merely a woman, yet
> Whose presence, power is
> Great as no goddess's
> Was deemèd, dreamèd; who
> This one work has to do --
> Let all God's glory through.

For Hopkins, in *May Magnificat*, May is Mary's month because then it is that mother nature best mirrors her in growth and beauty.

> All things rising, all things sizing
> Mary sees, sympathising
> With that world of good,
> Nature's motherhood.

There is an old saying among mothers, 'When young, your child makes your arms ache, when he grows up, he makes your heart ache.'

Mary may have sensed in Bethlehem that her Son's life would not be without pain. She would have been certain of it after old Simeon told her that Jesus would be a sign of contradiction and that a sword would pierce her own heart.

In *Resurrection: an Easter Sequence* by Northern Ireland poet W. R. Rogers, Jesus crucified, seeing his mother standing at the foot of the cross, remembers the happy days in Galilee when she called him from play. For her part, she muses, if only she had been more masterly with him would he then

> Have been like other men, a flat satisfied plain?
> But no. In him mountains of onlyness rose
> Snow-high. Dayspring was in his eyes
> At midnight. And he would not come down
> From his purpose even for her who was
> The root that had raised him to this Cross and crown
> Of thorns. Yet tenderly he spoke
> Goodbye now, his voice choking and dry.
> And as she went away, leaving him to die,
> The vast moon of his cry rose up upon the darkness.
> His heart broke …

On Calvary, Mary must have wonderd why the One whom she knew to be so good was suffering so much at the hands of people whom he loved.

Visitors to St Peter's in Rome will have seen Michelangelo's *Pietà*, the Italian for Pity. To symbolise the purity of Mary, he chose a single slab of Carrara marble without one black vein in it. He was twenty-four when he finished it in 1500. Some refused to believe that a mere youth could turn marble into this masterpiece of soft flesh. He, therefore, crept down one night into St Peter's and carved his name on Mary's sash, the only time he signed any of his works.

His *Pietà* shows a young man struck down in his youth and a mother not elderly and broken by suffering but herself young and serene. Mother and Son are entwined to show the deep bond between them. Their repose points to resurrection.

A poem called *Pietà* expresses Mary's bewilderment as the world gives back into her arms the Son whom she first gave it thirty-three years before in Bethlehem.

This man was once a little boy in my embrace,
his lovely face
was full of grace.
I loved him so,
How could a simple woman know
One day he'd die
'twixt earth and sky?
Oh, why crucify my son?
He was a friend to everyone.

This man was once a little boy in my embrace,
his lovely face
was full of grace.
He did no wrong,
But only good his whole life long.

He was the Light
That banished night.
The blind and sick he healed,
His mercy was God's Love revealed.

This man was once a little boy in my embrace,
his lovely face
was full of grace.
He gave a sign,
He turned Life's water into wine,
He was the Bread
On which we fed.
A man so kind, so good,
How could they nail him to the wood?

This man was once a little boy in my embrace,
his lovely face
was full of grace.
I weep for this,
His wounds in hands and feet I kiss,
And in his side,
This gash so wide.
I trust though he be slain
Our God will raise him up,
will raise him up
will raise him up again.

Léon Bloy had a great devotion to Our Lady of Sorrows.
He used to say, 'The only tragedy in life is not to be a saint.'
One of his prose poems was to Mary Immaculate:

I possess nothing but my sufferings
And you know how great they have been.
I offer you this unique treasure
Like a bunch of sorrowing flowers.
Already old and maybe close to death,
I offer you on my knees
My eyes and heart in tears,
In my extreme distress,
For you to take pity on me and mine;
I beg you, Mother of Jesus in Agony,
By the Seven Swords of your awesome Compassion,
Obtain for us the grace to be saints.

An old tradition, supported by Pope John Paul II, is that on Easter Day Jesus appeared first to the Virgin. Rainer Maria Rilke witnessed to this in his *Consolation of Mary with the Risen Christ*:

What they felt then, he and she, is it not
Sweeter than all mysteries
Though part of the earth,
When he, with the light pallor of the grave,
Came, free of all his burdens, to meet her
And be resurrected everywhere?

She was the first he came to. Beyond all words
Were they healed.
Yes, that is how both felt, healed. No need for them
To firmly touch each other.
For only a second he laid
His hand, soon to be eternal, on her womanly shoulder.
And they began,

Still as trees in springtime,
In an eternal togetherness,
This new season
Of fathomless communion.

George Mackay Brown (1921-96) was the poetic genius of
the Orkney Islands. Late in life, he gave up his allegiance to
a strict Scottish Calvinism to embrace the warmth and
colour of Catholicism.

In his poem *New Child* (1993), he tells the new-born Emma
Catherine Lawson: 'Wait a while, small voyager/ On the
shore, with seapinks and shells.' Emma must slowly learn
the names of the golden light, the sun, and the silvery-lit
moon; she must call 'the beautiful small splinters/ That
wet the stones, rain,' and the daisies that spill through her
fingers at night, stars.

The boat that will carry her on her life's voyage is still a-
building. 'A tree is growing/ That will be a tall mast.' Soon
enough, the voyage of Emma to the Land of Youth and
beyond will begin.

The final line, simple and solitary, is a moving prayer to
Mary:

Star of the Sea, shine on her voyage.

7. Ancient Poems about Mary

The tradition of writing poems about Mary goes back to the early days of Christianity but in the Middle Ages thousands of songs and poems were written in her honour. None is lovelier than a 15th century English poem *I Sing of a Maiden*.

He came all so still
Where his mother was,
As dew in April
That falleth on the grass.

He came all so still
To his mother's bower
As dew in April
That falleth on the flour

He came all so still
Where his mother lay,
As dew in April
That falleth on the spray.

Mother and maiden
Was never none but she;
Well may such a lady
God's mother be.

Another poem of the period is almost as beautiful:

> My heart knows well she is mine own
> To praise, this holy maiden,
> Who unto us has always shown
> A humble life and won a throne,
> Whose love unwearying has flown
> To comfort hearts grief-laden.
>
> I beg thee, Christ, thine ear incline
> To hear my adoration
> In honour of that mother thine
> Who ever blest must shine and shine,
> The bluest sky, the peerless shrine
> Of God's own vast creation.

A 13th century French poem is called *The Praises of Our Lady*:

> Red rose of a summer's day,
> Sweetest flower, soothe, I pray,
> Heart of mine that falls asleep.
> Perfume all my nights and days,
> Shield me and my spirits raise
> When I'm hurt and when I weep.
>
> Lady, ever rich in love
> Gentle as a turtle dove
> Light my path when darkness falls,
> Mother merciful and strong,
> Never far though I do wrong
> Hear this sinner when he calls.

Lady, watchful, sweet and kind,
Lead me on for I am blind,
Help me when I'm lost for breath.
When in fear I near my end
Stay close, Mother, dearest friend,
And bless me with a holy death.

A 13th Celtic poem, far more romantic, is called *Mary of the Gleaming Face:*

Blue-eyed, gleaming, is your face,
with dark-ridged eyes over it
fair-branching, slender is your hand
I owe a poem that does not lie
Pure, wholesome, yellow hair,
a vine of curls around your head
round, thin-fingered, pure palm,
O firm well-shaped foot
O curled, ridged yellow hair,
Mary of slender brows
give me no other judge
but the welcome of your heart
Let us feast on your shapely figure
– swift, mighty – side by side
Accept my best poems and songs
bright-languid, noble, decorous one
No woman but you in my home
its mistress may you be
False women and all the wealth I see
none of mine will pay them heed
Turn toward me your sole and palm

and your brown hair in beauty,
Your keen green young round eye
– may I fall in feast on your moist locks!

Another 13th century *Hymn To The Virgin* uses Latin words
and phrases of which the following are rough translations:
Velut Maris Stella, Like the Star of the Sea. *Parens et Puella*,
Mother and Maid. *Tam pia*, So Holy art thou. *Eva peccatrice*,
Eve the sinner. *De te genetrice*, Thou his Mother. *Salutis*,
Salvation. *Virtutis*, Virtue. *Rosa sine spina*, Rose without a
thorn. *Electa*, God's elect. *Effecta*, Made so by God.

Thou who art so fair and bright
Velut Maris Stella,
Brighter than the day is light,
Parens et puella,
I cry to thee, O seest me,
Lady, pray thy Son for me,
Tam pia,
That I might come to thee,
Maria.

All this world was lost and wild,
Eva peccatrice,
Till you bore the heavenly child,
De te genetrice.
At thine Ave there went away
The darkness followed by the day
Salutis,
The well at which we drink and play
Virtutis

Sweet Lady, flower of everything,
Rosa sine spina.
Bearer of Jesus, Heaven's King,
Gratia divina.
Mary, lift thy shining eyes,
Lady, Queen of Paradise
Electa.
Maid and Mother, God's best prize,
Effecta.

Another poem of the same period speaks of Mary as a Rose with five branches. One of them brightens Christmas Day, another frightens the devil in hell and so on. It has the eloquent refrain, 'Of a Rose, a lovely Rose,/ Of a Rose is all my song.' Here are three of its verses:

Hear me, ye old, and hear me, young,
Whence this brightest Rose has sprung,
None so fair as this fair Rose
Not since the world's begun.
Of a Rose, a lovely Rose,
Of a Rose is all my song.

Branches five of the Rose I've seen,
Lovelier Rose has never been,
From whose bosom Blossom sprang,
Rose, O Rose our heav'nly Queen.
Of a Rose, a lovely Rose,
Of a Rose is all my song.

Our shield is she, we need not cower,
She who bore the blessed Flower,
She our only strength and hope
In our dreaded final hour.
Of a Rose, a lovely Rose,
Of a Rose is all my song.

Lo, A Rose Forever Blooming is the translation of a 15th century
German poem:

Lo, a Rose for ever blooming
From tender stem hath sprung!
Of Jesse's lineage coming,
As those of old have sung.
A Rose came red and bright,
Amid the cold of winter,
When half-spent was the night.

This Rose with fragrance tender
And sweetness fills the air,
Dispels with glorious splendour
The darkness everywhere.
True man and yet true God,
From sin and death he saves us
And the earth which he has trod.

Isaiah it was foretold it,
The Rose I have in mind;
Chaste Mary's arms enfold it,
The Virgin Mother kind.
To show God's love and light,
She bore to us a Saviour,
When half-spent was the night.

There is always plenty of terror in lullabies and children's nursery rhymes. Think of *Rockabye Baby* or the equally frightening German lullaby *Schlaf, Kindlein, schlaf*:

Sleep, baby, sleep,
Thy Daddy minds his sheep,
Thy Mummy shakes a little tree
And shakes a dream down just for thee,
Sleep, baby, sleep.

Sleep, baby, sleep,
Outside there are two sheep,
One sheep is black and one is white,
And when thine eyes are not shut tight,
The black sheep comes and takes a bite,
Sleep, baby, sleep.

According to an anonymous 15th century Welsh poet, Mary sang God lullabies. As another put it, Jesus kept 'smiling upon his smiling mother's face'. Like any first-time mother, Mary had her hopes and fears and needed to voice them. In old English songs, she sings 'lulley', the early form of lullaby, to her baby Son.

Lulley, my Beloved, my dear Son, my sweeting,
Lulley, dear Heart, my own dear Darling.

Sometimes, mother and child talk to one another. Mary, distressed that her son has nothing but hay for his bed, asks how best she can please him. The Babe replies:

Mary, Mother, I pray ye,
Pick me up aloft, and in thine arm
Lap me tight till I am warm,

And dance me frequently.
And if I weep
And will not sleep,
Then sing me bye, bye, lully, lulley.

In some lullabies, Mary tries to soothe the grief of her child
only to hear him speak of his sufferings to come. In one
song, Mary foresees all the terrible things that might hap-
pen to her son in medieval times, including being snatched
by a falcon and ending his days dying like a knight.

Lully, lullay, lully, lullay;
The falcon hath born my child away.
He bore him up, he bore him down,
He bore him into an orchard brown.

In that orchard there was a hall,
Hung with purple and sable pall,
And in that hall there was a bed,
Curtained and draped with gold so red,
And in that bed there lieth a knight,
With wounds a-bleeding day and night.
A ceaseless vigil a lone maid keeps,
She kneeleth by his bed and weeps.

A similar 17th century Welsh poem is a dialogue between
Jesus and Mary called *Mary's Dream:*

'Mary, mother, dost thou sleep?'
'Yes, my child, and dream of thee.'
'Mother dear, but thou dost weep, –
Mother dear, what dost thou see?'
'Child, I see thee compassed round,

See thee taken, see thee bound,
On a cross I see thee tied,
See a spear-head pierce thee through,
See the blood break from thy side' –
'Mother dear, the dream is true.'

Whoso'er these words aright
Three times o'er shall say each night,
No ill dreams shall vex his bed,
Hell's dark land he ne'er shall tread.

A 15th century English lament called *Quia Amore Langueo* is spoken by Mary on Calvary. Often called *The Virgin's Complaint*, it might also be translated as *And All Because I Love Thee So*.

Within a room inside a tower,
While gazing on the moon stood I,
I saw a sweet Queen crowned with power
Upon a golden throne on high.
She made lament, with bitter cry,
For man whose soul by sin fell low:
I cannot bear to leave thee die,
Quia amore langueo.
And all because I love thee so.

I plead for love of man, my brother,
And beg him with a mother's cries.
What else to do, I am his mother,
What mother does her child despise?
If still thy flesh keeps falling low,
I still will grieve until thou rise,
And all because I love thee so.

Mother of Mercy was I made
To bring thee help, to thee illume,
For ever prompt to bring thee aid
Though thou art sunk in deepest gloom.
In my fond heart there is no room
To turn my face from friend or foe,
Or leave thee lonely to thy doom.
And all because I love thee so.

My Son hath suffered out of love,
His heart was opened with a spear.
To lift thy soul to heaven above
For thee he suffered, suffered here.
Doubt not thou art to him so dear.
And since my Son hath loved thee so
All of thy prayers I too will hear,
And all because I love thee so.

A poem from about 1450 called *An Appeal To All Mothers* is
put on Mary's lips. As she sings her final lullaby to her dead
Son, now cradled in her arms, she pleads with other mothers
to witness how fortunate they are compared with her.

Of all women that ever were born,
Who bearest children, stay and see
How my Son lieth so forlorn
Upon my lap, straight from the tree.

Your children dance upon your knee
With laughing, kissing and merry cheer.
Behold my child, behold now me,
For now liest dead my son, my dear.

Now that Mary is assumed into heaven, every soul that
enters Paradise, according to Dante, first turns his face to
hers:

> First look with care
> On her fair face,
> What thou wilt see
> Will thee prepare
> To see Christ's face
> Most gracefully
> Reflected there.

8. The Rosary:
The World's Favourite Prayer

Patrick Peyton, an Irish-American, was known as the Rosary Priest. He was born on 9 January 1909 in Carracastle in the parish of Attymass, Co Mayo, twenty miles from Knock. The sixth of nine children, he was brought up in a three-room thatched cottage which he called a little church because every day the rosary was recited at the hearth.

In 1928, aged 19, he emigrated to America where, a year before his ordination, he contracted TB. He put his cure down to Mary's prayers. He fulfilled his boyhood dream when he was ordained as a Holy Cross Father on June 15, 1941.

A year later, during World War II, he started a Rosary Crusade. 'I thought,' he said, 'of millions of people praying the rosary together for the end of the war, and peace being maintained by the worldwide practice of the family rosary.'

After beginning on local radio, he managed, against all odds, to get an hour of free air-time coast to coast. His first nationwide Family Rosary programme was scheduled for Mothers' Day 13 May 1945, eight days after the war ended. But who would star on it?

He called Bing Crosby in Hollywood. Will you help? 'Sure,' said Bing, 'tell me what to say.' Fr Peyton built the programme around the Sullivans, a family from Iowa. Five sons aged 20 to 28, whose motto was 'We Stick Together', were all killed when their cruiser *USS Juneau* was sunk by a Japanese sub in the battle for Guadalcanal. This was the greatest single sacrifice by any family in World War II. The papers agreed that the Family Rosary spot was the most touching of all the VE day programmes.

In time, with billboards all across America advertising it, 300 stars took part in the Family Theatre radio programmes. Among them were Gregory Peck, James Stewart, Jimmy Durant and Lucille Ball.

Each programme ended with Fr Peyton's twin slogans: 'The family that prays together, stays together' and 'A world at prayer is a world at peace.' As soon as TV became more popular than radio, Fr Peyton switched to that.

He also took his crusade on tour, visiting 40 countries, from the UK and Ireland to Australia and New Zealand. In 1964, in Sao Paulo, Brazil, he attracted 2 million people.

In 1987, realising his strength was waning, he said, 'God has given me a signal in my old age that this effort will not die, but will prosper. All that I've done so far is make the runway.'

In 1991 he celebrated his Golden Jubilee as a priest and returned to Attymass to celebrate it. He died the following June at the age of 83 in San Pedro, California. His last words were, 'Mary, my Queen, my Mother.'

His ministry went on through the Holy Cross Family Ministries. They look after the Family Rosary Campaign, produce movies through Family Theatre Productions, distribute two million Rosary beads each year and support family life in developing countries.

Faithful to his roots, each year Fr Peyton made a pilgrimage to Our Lady's shrine at Knock. It was fitting that on June 3, 2001, the cause of his beatification was announced at the Rosary Rally in Knock. On 16 October 2002, Pope John Paul, in his Apostolic Letter on the Rosary, quoted Fr Peyton's famous phrase, 'The family that prays together stays together.'

The rose was the first flower to be cultivated and fossils over 30 million years old have been found. It was so beautiful that Cleopatra received Mark Antony in her palace, knee-deep in a sea of roses.

The rosary which Fr Peyton made so popular means 'Crown of Roses'. Since it is the crown of flowers, each Hail Mary is part of a crown of roses and the rosary is the rose of all devotions.

In the rosary we meditate on the mysteries of joy, sorrow and glory of Jesus and Mary. It's a prayer said to and with the mother of God. She joins her unfailing prayer to ours. The miracle of Cana proved Jesus can never turn down a request from her.

In every recent apparition, Mary invited us to say the rosary to bring peace to us and the world. For example, Our Lady of Fatima, on each appearance, said, 'Pray the rosary every day.'

Popes have all recommended this devotion:

Pius IX: 'Give me an army saying the rosary and I will conquer the world.'

Leo XIII: 'The Rosary is the root of all our blessings. There is no more excellent way of praying.'

St Pius X: 'The Rosary is the most beautiful and the richest of all prayers to the Mediatrix of all grace; it is the prayer that touches most the heart of the Mother of God. Say it every day.'

Pius XI: 'If you desire peace in your hearts, in your homes, and in your country, gather each evening to recite the Rosary, no matter how burdened you may be with work and cares.'

Pius XII: 'There is no surer means of calling down God's blessings upon the family than the daily recitation of the Rosary.

John XXIII: 'The Rosary is the glory of the Roman church. In the minds of the faithful it takes its place after the Mass and the sacraments. We say it in its entirety every single day of the year, for it is the best way to pray and meditate.'

The saints follow the popes. It is hard to find a picture of Blessed Teresa of Calcutta without her Rosary. Once when she was on a talk show, a strange sound kept coming over the mike. She was fingering her beads even while she was being interviewed.

Padre Pio, now St Pio of Pietrelcina, was the first priest ever to have the stigmata. He is the Spiritual Father of The Blue Army in America which is dedicated to Our Lady of Fatima and follows her request to pray the Rosary each day.

Pictures show Padre Pio laughing while his right hand is hidden in his breast pocket. He is saying his Rosary to Mary whom he spoke of as 'my dear little Mother' and 'Mother of all mothers'.

When a friar asked him if Our Lady ever appeared in his room, he answered, 'When was she ever not in my room?'

He could do three things at once, he said, and one of them was always saying his Rosary. When someone asked him to draw up a plan of prayer, he responded, with a shrug, 'My child, the holy Rosary.' One of his most popular pieces of advice was, 'Love the Madonna and pray the Rosary, for her Rosary is the weapon against the evil of the modern world.'

Moments before he died, aged 81, still clutching his Rosary, he said, 'Jesus! Mary!', then, according to his superior, his head fell gently to his chest and 'he died like a little bird'.

Many an old lady is proud of her Rosary. It may have simple wooden beads, it may show signs of frequent mending. But often it is cherished because, for more than a century, it was handed on from one woman in the family to another, their supple fingers becoming slowly arthritic over the years. How many hundreds of thousands of Aves have been said on it, in many holy places – in churches and chapels, before Mary's local statues, in places of pilgrimage like Guadalupe, Fatima and Lourdes?

Tennyson wrote, 'More things are wrought by prayer/ Than this world dreams of.' If so, how many blessings has this line of devoted women brought upon their families, their friends and the whole world?

The Rosary probably began in Irish monasteries over a thousand years ago. When the monks chanted the 150 psalms of David every day, lay helpers wanted to join in but they hadn't the time or the Latin. Around the year 800, they adapted the monks' prayers to their own needs.

Every time the monks chanted a psalm, they said the Lord's Prayer. To make sure they kept up, they carried 150 pebbles in a pouch, then they made 150 knots in a piece of string. With the Celtic infatuation with the number three, the prayer rope was reduced to 50 knots to be said three times.

When Irish monks began to evangelise Europe, they took this devotion with them. In the 11th century, priests and people began to respond to the psalms by reciting the first part of the Hail Mary, called the Angelic Salutation which makes up the first part of the Ave. This prayer, said 150 times, was known as Mary's Psalter.

Over the centuries the devotion developed into the Rosary as we know it. The Angelic Salutation was extended to what we now call the Hail Mary. There are five tens (or decades) on a Rosary, to be said three times with a mystery attached to each decade. An Our Father precedes each decade and a Glory Be at the end honours the Trinity.

The basic idea has never changed: the prayer represents a spiritual bouquet of roses offered to the Virgin Mary so that with her help we may become more like her Son and more devoted to the Trinity. Hence this concluding prayer:

Pray for us, O Holy Mother of God.

That we may be made worthy of the promises of
Christ.

Let us pray.

O God, whose only-begotten Son, by his life, death, and resurrection, has purchased for us the rewards of eternal life, grant, we beseech thee, that meditating upon these mysteries of the Most Holy Rosary of the Blessed Virgin Mary, we may imitate what they contain and obtain what they promise, through the same Christ our Lord. Amen.

In 1595, St Pius V put the Rosary in the form we are used to. Two years later, he asked the faithful to pray the Rosary to save Catholic Europe from the threat of Islam. On 7 October, 1571, an allied Catholic fleet defeated the Turks. Chesterton celebrated this famous victory in his poem *The Battle of Lepanto* with its opening lines, 'White founts falling in the Courts of the sun, / And the Soldan of Byzantium is smiling as they run.' Pius V commemorated the victory with the feast of Our Lady of the Rosary on 7 October.

The Joyful Mysteries (on Mondays and Thursdays) are the Annunciation; the Visitation of Mary to her cousin, Elizabeth; the Nativity; the Presentation of the child Jesus in the Temple; the Finding of the child Jesus in the Temple. The Sorrowful Mysteries (on Tuesdays and Fridays) are the Agony in the Garden; the Scourging at the pillar; the Crowning with thorns; the Carrying of the Cross; the Crucifixion.

The Glorious Mysteries (on Wednesdays, Saturdays and Sundays) are the Resurrection; the Ascension; the Descent of the Holy Spirit; the Assumption of Mary; the Coronation of Mary in Heaven.

On October 16th, 2002, to mark the 24th anniversary of his election as Pope, John Paul II made the first changes to the Rosary in over 500 years. He proposed five more decades to emphasise Christ's ministry.

He reminds us that 'to recite the Rosary is nothing other than to contemplate with Mary the face of Christ' who is 'the light of the world' (Jn 8:12).

The Mysteries of Light are these: The Baptism of Our Lord. (Matthew 3:13-17) The Wedding at Cana. (John 2: 1-11.) The Proclamation of the Kingdom. (Mark 1:14-15) The Transfiguration. (Matthew 17:1-8.) The Institution of the Eucharist. (Matthew 26:26-28)

The Pope suggests that the second weekly meditation on the joyful mysteries be moved to Saturday, leaving Thursday free for meditating on the Mysteries of Light.

His *Letter on the Rosary* sums up his love of the Blessed Virgin. From the beginning, he placed his Petrine ministry under her protection with his motto, *Totus Tuus,* I Am All Thine. He explained on the 50th anniversary of his ordination that he had learned this prayer from de Montfort's treatise on *The True Devotion to Mary* and it had guided him from his student days. On the 160th anniversary of its publication in 2004, he wrote, 'My motto, *Totus tuus*, is inspired by the doctrine of St Louis-Marie Grignion de Monfort. These two words express total abandonment to Jesus through Mary.'

Two weeks after his election as Pope, he admitted: 'The Rosary is my favourite prayer. A marvellous prayer! Marvellous in its simplicity and its depth.'

He once asked, 'Would you like me to tell you a secret? It is simple and, really, no secret at all: Pray, pray hard. Say the Rosary every day. How beautiful is the family that recites the Rosary in the evening.'

One of John Paul's proudest moments was on 10 October 1982 when he canonised his compatriot Fr Maximilian Kolbe. The saint had been devoted to Mary since his first communion at the age of twelve. That day, he asked her what would become of him.

> She came to me holding two crowns, one white, the other red. She asked if I was willing to accept either of these crowns. The white one meant that I should persevere in purity, and the red that I should become a martyr. I said that I would accept them both.

On 17 February 1941, he was sent to the Pawiak prison in Warsaw where he was singled out for punishment because he wore a rosary on his Franciscan habit. An SS guard asked him repeatedly if he believed in Christ. Each time he answered, 'Yes,' the guard hit him till he lost consciousness.

On 28 May 1941, he was moved to Auschwitz and branded Prisoner 16670. In July, when there was an escape from the camp, retribution was exacted. Ten men were to be put to death for each escapee. When NCO, Francis Gajowniczek, married with young children, was among the ten chosen, he cried out, 'O my poor wife, my poor children. I shall never see them again.'

Maximilian volunteered to take his place. He was led off with the rest to an underground bunker where they were given no food or water.

Eye-witness Bruno Borgowiec reported that in the bunker the victims kept on saying the rosary and singing hymns to Mary. It was, he said, like being in church.

As the days passed, their prayers were reduced to a whisper. When most were too weak to raise themselves off the floor, Fr Kolbe remained kneeling or standing in the centre, smiling at the SS guards.

Three weeks passed with the prisoners dying one by one, until only Fr Kolbe was left. To finish him off, he was given an injection of carbolic acid. He offered his arm to the executioner with a prayer on his lips.

After his body was burned in the ovens, his ashes were scattered. Mary had kept her promise and given Fr Kolbe two crowns, white and red.

9. The Rosary in Ireland

The Rosary that began during the ninth century in Irish monasteries, was never more needed than in 1540 when Henry VIII began to persecute the church in Ireland.

The local Parliament established the monarch's supremacy over the church and abolished papal rule. Religious houses were closed down, monasteries and churches fell into ruins. Many priests and lay people died professing their faith. Even invoking Mary's name made the Irish ineligible for public office or the professions.

Augustine Birrell, Britain's Chief Secretary to Ireland during the Easter Rising of 1916, wrote that the Irish 'tenacity of faith is, I believe, unexampled in the history of the whole world'. Until the reign of Queen Victoria, a Catholic in Ireland was an outcast. 'Catholics,' said Birrell, 'were robbed of their lands; they were given their choice between hell and Connacht.'

But they did not yield. And their love for Mary, the Mother of the Golden Heights, helped them survive persecution.

In the early 18th century, the scaled-down Irish Penal Rosary, little more than a few beads on a string, became popular. It was a small secret sign of local rebellion against the English religion. The crucifix was hidden in the hand or slipped up the sleeve. At the end of it was a ring, and this ring was moved from the thumb to the four fingers, one after the other, in order to recite the decades of the rosary. Various symbols were etched on the rosary, a hammer for the nails of the cross, a chalice represented the Last Supper, a ladder pointed the way to heaven and so on.

The rosary continued to play a major role in the history of Ireland. In Sean O'Casey's *The Plough and the Stars,* Fluther complains about the British soldier who wanted the Irish to fight fair. 'Fight fair! A few hundhred scrawls o' chaps with a couple of guns an' Rosary beads, again' a hundhred thousand thrained men with horse, fut, an' artillery ... an' he wants us to fight fair!'

Those were the odds during the Rising in 1916. The home-made bombs of the Volunteers threatened themselves more than the Crown forces but they had other weapons. On the roof of the Dublin GPO, every half hour, men thumbed the Rosary with their rifle in their other hand until the Friday when the place went up in flames. They machine-gunned the enemy with Hail Marys.

On the first night of the Rising, de Valera was checking up on his command around Boland's Mill when he came across his men, on their knees in the dark, reciting the Rosary. He joined them in spirit for a decade before moving on to check on the sentries further along the railway embankment. He gave the pass-word. No reply. The sentries were praying with the others. He pointed out that sentries were not to leave their posts for any reason, not even the Rosary.

When Pearse's order of surrender was delivered to Hanlon's fish market where Clarke, Connolly and McDermott were taking refuge, the men under their command knelt down. Rifles in one hand, beads in the other, they said the Rosary.

The leaders of the Rising were comforted by their beads as they awaited execution in Kilmainham Jail.

Thomas McDonagh was wearing his mother's Rosary round his neck when he was shot in the Stonebreakers' Yard. His sister, a nun, was given it afterwards. A few beads had been shot away. The restored Rosary is on exhibit in Kilmainham Museum.

When Father Augustine, a Capuchin, visited John McBride in his death cell, McBride tugged his Rosary out of his pocket, his final gift to his mother.

Michael Mallin was, as it were, handcuffed by his Rosary, when his wife and children visited him in Kilmainham on Sunday, May 7.

Father Albert wrote of that night, 'Having visited Con Colbert and Eamon Kent, I went to Sean Heuston's cell at about 3.20 a.m. He was kneeling beside a table, with his Rosary beads in his hands.'

Thomas Kent was executed in Cork. Afterwards, blood-spattered in his hand was the Rosary given him by the prison chaplain, Fr Sexton.

When the Rising was over and prisoners were being transported to England, the men recited the Rosary together in the locked hold. A storm blew up. Many prayed to Mary they'd sink and be drowned in preference to sea-sickness.

Most were interned in Frongoch in North Wales. Whatever the routine, one thing never changed. In each hut, after the Last Post sounded at 9.30, the men knelt at the end of their beds to say the Rosary. This ritualised, almost hypnotic form of prayer was their link with home. Though it sounded like the distant sound of a cattle auction, it reminded them of their Irishness and their loved ones back home.

Later, on 1 November 1920, young Kevin Barry, who had shot a British soldier, was about to be hanged in Mountjoy. The other prisoners, having kept silent all night to let him sleep, said the Rosary aloud for him at 7.15.

Michael Collins had ordered that 'there would be no more lonely scaffolds in our time'. Hence, in the first light of morning, Dubliners made their way to the gates of Mountjoy Prison. Women clutching Rosary beads and bare-headed men holding prayer books gathered to pay their respects to the youth about to die.

With British planes circling overhead and armoured cars patrolling the streets, a large group of the Republican women's organisation, Cumann na mBan, arrived from St Stephen's Green, adding their prayers to those of the crowd already gathered.

At 8 o'clock, as the prison bell began to toll, they fell to their knees. The police ordered them in vain to disperse. They said the Five Sorrowful Mysteries. Soon, an official posted a notice on the prison gate. 'The sentence of law passed on Kevin Barry, found guilty of murder, was carried into execution at 8 o'clock this morning.'

Ernie O'Malley, author of the classic book, *On Another Man's Wound,* was using the alias of Stewart when he was captured by British Auxiliaries in December 1920. In his pocket were his beads. He needed them. Often during the Tan War and, later, during the Civil War, he would return frozen from manoeuvres, only to have to wait outside the cottage till the host family finished the Rosary with all the trimmings. The final three Hail Marys for Ireland meant a hot meal was – at long last – not far away.

O'Malley's funniest incident occurred in October 1920. He and Kevin Lynch, two of the fiercest of guerrilla fighters, were billeted on an old Fenian and his son. Having spent the day in the hills, the hardest part was to come: the Rosary, recited kneeling on the stone floor. It took hours, or seemed to. Finally, the host and his son left the kitchen to share a bed in a bedroom.

Through the open door came the drone of still unfinished business. The old man was ploughing through the Litany of Our Lady. 'House of Gold, Ark of the Covenant.' There was a pause as the old man said, 'Move up in the bed there, Patsy.' The exhausted son must have dozed off. 'Patsy, move up, I tell ye.' Still no response. 'Patsy, take in your fat arse out of that. Now, Gate of Heaven, Morning Star ...'

Lynch and O'Malley stuffed the ends of the blankets into their mouths to stop themselves roaring.

The Colditz story was anticipated in 1921 when prisoners were interned in the Rath camp on the Curragh. They dug 'Brady's tunnel', named after Jim Brady of Cavan, a former coal-miner. He and another had worked miracles with only a screw driver and a crowbar. Sandy soil had to be removed in pillow cases and sprinkled under the floorboards of the huts.

With the tunnel finished, the escape began. First went two men with wirecutters for the perimeter fence. Dubliners followed, then a dozen from Roscommon. But a greedy Longford man had brought a suitcase with him. It banged against the pit-props, causing them to collapse.

They planned to head west for the Curragh racecourse. Unfortunately, at the tunnel exit, there was a blanket of fog. They broke up into small groups but kept banging into one another. They'd been walking in circles. The Roscommon men did the only sensible thing. Kneeling beside a barbed-wire fence, they said the Rosary. It worked.

No sooner were the trimmings over than they heard rooks in nearby trees. The only trees near the camp were behind the Curragh Grand Stand. They followed the cawing to the racecourse and thence to freedom.

The strangest and most moving appearance of the Rosary in Irish history took place the day after Michael Collins, Commander-in-Chief of the Free State Army, was shot dead. The news spread quickly to Kilmainham Jail.

Tom Barry, one of the Republican prisoners, never forgot

the eerie silence that settled over the jail. He chanced to look down from the corridor above. In the large ground-floor assembly area, what looked like a thousand hard-bit-ten Republican prisoners had fallen to their knees. And he heard the familiar drum-roll of the Rosary for the repose of the soul of Michael Collins, their enemy and their friend.

10. Mary's Many Titles

Mary has many titles, 'Lady of Flowers, New Rose, Bright Red Rose, Lady of Mercy, Star of the Sea,' and a thousand more. Each of us has his or her own preferences.

But there are certain key titles such as: Mother of God *(Theotokos),* Mother of the Church, Universal Mother, Mary Immaculate, Mary Ever Virgin, Second Eve, Mary Mediatrix of All Grace, Mary Assumed into Heaven, Comforter of the Afflicted.

Some of her titles are gathered into a kind of floral bouquet called a Litany. The one we are most familiar with is the Litany of Loreto.

Lord have mercy on us.
Lord have mercy on us.
Christ have mercy on us.
Christ have mercy on us.
Lord have mercy on us.
Lord have mercy on us.
Christ, hear us.
Christ, graciously hear us.
God the Father of Heaven, *have mercy on us.*
God the Son, Redeemer of the world, *have mercy on us.*
God the Holy Ghost, *have mercy on us.*
Holy Trinity, one God, *have mercy on us.*
Holy Mary, *pray for us*

Holy Mother of God,
Holy Virgin of virgins,
Mother of Christ,
Mother of divine grace,
Mother most pure,
Mother most chaste,
Mother inviolate,
Mother undefiled,
Mother most amiable,
Mother most admirable,
Mother of good counsel,
Mother of our Creator,
Mother of our Redeemer,
Virgin most prudent,
Virgin most venerable,
Virgin most renowned,
Virgin most powerful,
Virgin most merciful,
Virgin most faithful,
Mirror of justice,
Seat of wisdom,
Cause of our joy,
Spiritual vessel,
Vessel of honour,
Singular vessel of devotion,
Mystical rose,
Tower of David,
Tower of ivory,
House of gold,

Ark of the covenant,

Gate of Heaven,

Morning Star,

Health of the sick,

Refuge of sinners,

Comforter of the afflicted,

Help of Christians,

Queen of Angels,

Queen of Patriarchs,

Queen of Prophets,

Queen of Apostles,

Queen of Martyrs,

Queen of Confessors,

Queen of Virgins,

Queen of all Saints,

Queen conceived without original sin,

Queen of the most holy Rosary,

Queen of peace,

Lamb of God, who takes away the sins of the world:
Spare us, O Lord.

Lamb of God, who takes away the sins of the world:
Graciously hear us, O Lord.

Lamb of God, who takes away the sins of the world:
Have mercy on us.

Pray for us, most holy Mother of God,
That we may be made worthy of the promises of Christ.

Let us pray. O God, whose only begotten Son, by his life,
death and resurrection has purchased for us the rewards

of eternal life, grant, we beseech you, that while meditating of the mysteries of the most holy Rosary of the Blessed Virgin Mary, we may imitate what they contain and obtain what they promise, through Christ our Lord. Amen.

A fine Gaelic litany from about 750 is entitled 'Myden Dheelish,' *(Maighdean Dílis),* Darling Virgin.

O Great Mary.

O Mary, greatest of Maries.

O Greatest of Women.

O Queen of Angels.

O Mistress of the Heavens.

O Woman replete with the grace of the Holy Ghost.

O Blessed and Most Blessed.

O Mother of Eternal Glory.

O Mother of the heavenly and earthly Church.

O Mother of Love and Indulgence.

O Mother of the Golden Heights.

O Honour of the Sky.

O Sign of Tranquillity.

O Gate of Heaven.

O Golden Casket.

O Couch of Love and Mercy.

O Temple of Divinity.

O Beauty of Virgins.

O Mistress of the Tribes.

O Fountain of the Parterres.

O Cleansing of the Sins.

O Purifying of Souls.

O Mother of Orphans.

O Breast of the Infants.

O Solace of the Wretched.

O Star of the Sea.

O Handmaid of the Lord.

O Mother of Christ.

O Resort of the Lord.

O Graceful like the Dove.

O Serene like the Moon.

O Resplendent like the Sun.

O Cancelling Eve's disgrace.

O Regeneration of Life.

O Beauty of Women.

O Leader of the Virgins.

O Enclosed Garden.

O Closely Locked Fountain.

O Mother of God.

O Perpetual Virgin.

O Holy Virgin.

O Prudent Virgin.

O Serene Virgin.

O Chaste Virgin.

O Temple of the Living God.

O Royal Throne of the Eternal King.

O Sanctuary of the Holy Ghost.

O Virgin of the Root of Jesse.

O Cedar of Mount Lebanon.

O Cypress of Mount Zion.

O Crimson Rose of the Land of Jacob.

O Blooming like the Palm Tree.

O Fruitful like the Olive Tree.

O Glorious Son-bearer.

O Light of Nazareth.

O Glory of Jerusalem.

O Beauty of the World.

O Noblest-Born of the Christian Flock.

O Queen of Life.

O Ladder of Heaven.

In a delightful poem, 'A Little Litany,' Chesterton (1874-1936) takes some of Mary's titles and shows how Jesus himself would have enjoyed them.

Star of his Morning; that unfallen star
In that strange starry overturn of space
When earth and sky changed places for an hour
And heaven looked upwards in a human face.

Or young on your strong knees and lifted up
Wisdom cried out, whose voice is in the street,
And more than twilight of twiformed cherubim
Made of his throne indeed a mercy-seat.

Or risen from play at your pale raiment's hem
God, grown adventurous from all time's repose,
Or your tall body climbed the Ivory Tower
And kissed upon your mouth the Mystic Rose.

No wonder Chesterton, who died in 1936, was named by Pius XI a 'Defender of the Catholic Faith'. Four centuries earlier, the Vatican had bestowed this title on a far less worthy recipient, Henry VIII.

In the Mozarabic Liturgy, we find many a poem made out of Mary's titles, as in this *Song For Our Lady's Assumption*:

As the tower of David art thou, O Mary,
And in thee there is no flaw,
How beautiful and lovely art thou in the adorning,
And the odour of thy ointments
Is like the fragrance of Libanus,
Above all perfume.
Like a dove brooding over swelling waters,
Like vials that pour out perfumed oil,
Like lilies distilling their fragrance,
Like the golden vessels of Tharsis,
Like the choice Libanus and the cedar tree,
Like fair tall columns of marble
Set upon bases of gold, art thou, O Mary!
How beautiful and how lovely!

A modern 'Hymn to Mary,' is woven out of a few of her many titles.

Ave Rosa Mundi
Rose without a thorn
Flower whose fragrance pleased God's Son
When he was born.

Ave Mater Dei
Mother of Our Lord
Underneath his Cross you felt
A cruel sword.

Ave Domus Pacis
God's own House of Peace
When you look upon our sorrows
They all cease.

Ave Virgo Clemens
Virgin sweet yet strong
Plead for us with your dear Son
When we do wrong.

Ave Maris Stella
Star who is our guide
Help us brave life's raging storms
And angry tide.

Ave Porta Coeli
Gate to Life through death
Pray for us both now and at
Our final breath.

'The New Eve,' an 11th century poem by an Irish monk, seemed in the tradition of the time to disparage all women in the person of Eve:

Great Adam's wife am I, my name is Eve,
The one who long ago made Jesus grieve.
Who stole sweet heaven from my children? Me.
I should be doomed to die upon the Tree.

Without my sin, no ice in any place,
No glistening wind to freeze the human race.
For rains, for gales, for snows, I am to blame.
All woes flow out of me, Eve is my name.

In her poem 'Eve' (1865), Christina Rossetti is no more forgiving. Eve speaks here in the person of the Mother Of All The Living.

I, Eve, sad mother
Of all who must live,
I, not another,
Plucked bitterest fruit to give
My friend, husband, lover.

Even the creatures of the field suffer because of Eve's disobedience:

The mouse paused in his walk
And he dropped his wheaten stalk;
Grave cattle wagged their heads
In rumination;
The eagle gave a cry
From his cloud station;
Larks on thyme beds
Forbore to mount or sing;
Bees drooped upon wing:
The raven perched on high
Forgot his ration;
The conies in their rock,
A feeble nation,
Quaked sympathetical;
The mocking bird left off to mock;
Huge camels knelt as if
In deprecation;
The kind hart's tears were falling;
Chattered the wistful stork;

> Dove-voices with a dying fall
> Cooed desolation
> Answering grief by grief.
> Only the serpent in the dust
> Wriggling and crawling,
> Grinned an evil grin and thrust
> His tongue out with its fork.

If women got a bad press from the sin of Eve, they were more than compensated in the goodness and innocence of the Virgin Mary, as shown in this ancient poem:

> Had not the apple taken been,
> The apple not been taken,
> Mary would not have been our Queen
> And we would feel forsaken
>
> Yet Adam's sin was good for us
> Though it deserved the rod
> For Christ died on the wood for us
> And for this we say, Thank God.
>
> O happy fault of Adam that brought us such a Redeemer. O happy fault of Eve that brought us Mary the Mother of Mercy.

Many writers have pointed out that the Latin word for Eve, *Eva,* is reversed in the *Ave* spoken to Mary by the Angel Gabriel. As Christ, the second Adam, reversed the work of the first Adam, Mary, the second Eve, reversed the work of the first Eve. In the minds of medieval Christians, Mary the Second Eve turned the wilderness back into a garden, giving Mary a new title, Our Lady Of The Flowers.

11. Our Lady of the Flowers

In earlier times, Christians named not only great cathedrals like Chartres and Paris after Mary but the humblest flowers of the field. This made sense, Fr Merton says, since Mary's Yes at the annunciation 'opens the door of created nature, of time, of history, to the Word of God. God enters into his creation.'

Christians first saw Mary prefigured in lush images from the Jewish Bible. She is a rose of Sharon, and a lily of the valley.

I have struck root among a glorious people,
Like a cedar on Lebanon,
Like a cypress on Mount Hermon,
Like a palm tree in Engedi,
Like a rosebush in Jericho,
Like a fair olive tree in a field,
Like a plain tree growing beside running water.
I give forth perfume,
I spread my branches,
I bud forth delights like a vine,
My blossoms bear fruit fair and rich.

For Venerable Bede in the 8th century, the Madonna lily's translucent white petals represented Mary's body as she was assumed into heaven, and its golden anthers, the radiance of her soul.

Four centuries later, St Bernard wrote:

> In the garden of his Mother
> God hath planted every flower
> That adorns his church:
> Violet of humility,
> Lily of purity,
> Rose of loving kindness.

From about the same period came an old French poem that says to Mary:

> A garden filled with flowers
> Of every fragrance,
> Your Son has made of you.

No wonder the old monastic gardens were little Edens and places of prayer. After all, had not the Master pointed to the lilies of the field, saying that not even Solomon in all his glory was arrayed like one of these?

In medieval poetry, Mary was lovelier than the lilies of the field. She was the flower of flowers, flower of virginity, flower of purity, changeless lily, mysterious rose, rose without a thorn, enclosed garden of the King of Heaven, a paradise garden carpeted with flowers.

St Francis was careful not to tread on any wayside flower, since it was a symbol of Mary, the Rose of Sharon. He left us a charming picture of friars crossing the land and spreading respect for all God's creatures, even the wild flowers which in their beauty encourage us to become instruments of God's peace.

When Francis was once asked, 'What would you do if you knew you would die tomorrow?' he answered, 'Keep on tending my garden.' Maybe this is why his statue is found in so many gardens.

This was the time of the Crusades when Christians turned their minds to the Holy Land as never before. Warriors and traders returned home with supposed relics of the Virgin. St Peter's shadow and Paul's handkerchief had healed the sick, why not, say, Mary's slipper? A tour of her relics throughout Europe in 1112 and England in 1113 worked many miracles and brought in the funds needed for church construction. Chartres Cathedral was built to house her tunic.

Since Mary was assumed into heaven, there were no bones among her relics, but in the simplicity of the time, the faithful honoured bits of her clothing, strands of her hair, even dried traces of her milk and her tears, all 'miraculously' preserved.

Plants and flowers were named after these relics, hence *Our Lady's Tresses, Our Lady's Mantle* and *Tears* and *Milk Drops* and *Our Lady's Slipper*.

The Slipper Chapel at Walsingham was so named because it housed the relic of Our Lady's Slipper. This in turn inspired the practice of pilgrims removing their footwear for the final walk to the main shrine.

Once the process of naming flowers after Mary began, there was no stopping it. And not just flowers and grasses but all the healing plants, too.

The first flower associated with the Virgin was *St Mary's Gold* or *Marigold*. Versatile and long-lasting, it was used in medicine against stings and in cooking as a bitter spice. Young women used it to dye their hair. Because it opens from mid-morning to mid-afternoon, Shakespeare in *The Winter's Tale* speaks of

> The Marigold that goes to bed wi' th' sun,
> And with him rises weeping.

In *Cymbeline*, he describes how

> Winking Mary-buds (*Marigolds*) begin
> To ope' their golden eyes.

Mary influenced the European spirit as Shakespeare influenced the English language. Every aspect of her life came into the naming of plants. There were several manger plants. *Holy Hay, Cradlewort* and *Our Lady's Bedstraw* had bloomed when her Son was placed on them. There were many milk plants, whose white spots were due to the Madonna's milk spattering them, for example, *Mary's Milkdrops'* and the milk thistle, known botanically as *Silybum Marianum*. These flowers may even have inspired the nursing Madonnas in religious art.

Wherever Christians noticed botanical specimens of fragility and delicacy, they named them after some aspect of the Virgin. Soon the whole countryside in its colours and perfumes seemed to be a shrine built by God to honour his mother.

In the tender words of a 13th century 'Song of Praise to Mary':

> Grass, flowers and clover join in praising her,
> Laughing roses and playing blossoms,
> Hedges in boom, rose blossoms and lily petals,
> Valleys of roses and fields of violets,
> And flowers that shine through the clover.

When the Dalai Lama visited Fatima in 2001, he honoured the Virgin by placing a flower at the feet of her statue in the Chapel of the Apparitions.

In many religions, the bliss of Paradise is centred on a garden as in the greatest of love poems, 'The Song of Songs'.

> My beloved speaks and says to me:
> Arise, my love, my fair one,
> and come away;
> for, lo, the winter is past,
> the rain is over and gone.
> The flowers appear on the earth,
> the time of singing has come,
> and the voice of the turtledove
> is heard in our land.
>
> Awake, O north wind,
> And come, O south wind!
> Blow upon my garden,
> let its fragrance be wafted abroad.
> Let my beloved come to his garden,
> and eat its choicest fruit.

Medieval monks called their flower gardens 'Paradises', from the Persian word meaning walled space. There they found peace of mind in the green fragments of a lost Eden. The sick convalesced there. Scholars set their desks in a central place where we might put a pool or fountain, reading and writing while inhaling the fragrance of the flowers. They never went in for close-cropped grass, their only mowers being sheep. They simply delighted in the beauty and the scented air.

In 1932, Frances Crane Lillie followed the monks' example and prepared the Garden of Our Lady on the grounds of St Joseph's Church, Woods Hole, Massachusetts. The idea spread of giving flowers their old Christian names and planting them in a special garden to bloom all year round in honour of the Virgin.

Mary's Gardens, liturgically blessed as of old, became a kind of year-round memorial to Our Lady. Gardens were seen again not just as restful and beautiful but as sacramental. They are holy places, the plants and flowers being gifts of God, the shape, colour and fragrance of each a mirror of Mary's life and a sign of the beauty of her soul.

Ireland's traditional devotion to Our Lady, *Muire Mháthair*, is to be seen in the National Mary Garden in Knock, County Mayo. Encouraged by the Director, Monsignor Horan, it was opened and blessed on the Feast of Corpus Christi, 1983. Consisting of eight beds, it is next to the Blessed Sacrament Chapel.

In the garden the visitor finds the loveliest of litanies, the flowers. It is a fine preparation for the Knock experience, that is, Mary's appearance with the Heavenly Lamb, Angels, St Joseph and St John on a wet Thursday evening, August 21st, 1879.

In 1986 the planting was revised by Br Sean MacNamara CFC, famous for cataloguing the plants of the Burren in County Clare. For fifteen years, he had researched the flowers of Our Lady in old Irish rural traditions. He documented over 150 Irish wildflowers for which Mary-names had been current in the religious traditions of the countryside, some thirty of which bore Mary's old Gaelic name, *Muire*.

In 1986, Br Sean increased the native wild flower varieties at Knock to eighty, taking at least two from source colonies in every county in Ireland. In general, white flowers symbolised Mary's joys, purple flowers her sorrows and yellow or gold flowers her glories. Here are a few examples:

Columbine – *Our Lady's Shoes*. Iris – *Mary's Sword*. Foxglove – *Our Lady's Gloves*. Narcissus – *Mary's Star*. Forget-me-not _ *Mary's Eyes*. Fuchsia – *Our Lady's Eardrops*. Lily-of-the-Valley – *Our Lady's Tears*. St John's Wort – *Mary's Glory*. Cuckoo Flower – *Lady's Smock*. Sweet Violet – *Our Lady's Modesty*. Golden Saxifrage – *Lady's Cushion*. Snowdrops – *Candlemas Bells*. Cornflower – *Mary's Crown*. Mullein – *Our Lady's Candle,* which calls to mind the lines:

> The Virgin Mary moves over the land
> With heaven's fire in her hand.

Flowers on the altar represent Mary's closeness to Christ.

But once, Mary, like the plants named after her, seemed to inhabit every wild and hidden place. Look under any bush, in any clump of grass, beside any stream, and you will find her.

Mary was most associated with the lily and the rose, no matter that the lilies growing wild which Jesus spoke of were probably anemones and the Rose of Sharon was a crocus or a narcissus. For Dante, Mary is 'The Rose in which the Word was made flesh.'

In the apparition at Guadalupe, her presence was made known by roses blooming on a peak in winter. At La Salette, near Grenoble, she wore three garlands of roses with tiny roses on her slippers. She brought roses with her at Lourdes, Pontmain, Pellevoisin, Beauraing and Banneaux.

When Pope John Paul II visited Knock in 1987, he gave the shrine a Golden Rose. For centuries it has been a special mark of a Pope's affection. It was a reminder of Mary appearing as Queen of the Most Holy Rosary with a crown and a golden rose. The Holy Father said:

> Here I am at the goal of my journey to Ireland: The Shrine of Our Lady of Knock. Since I first learnt of the centenary of this shrine, I have felt a strong desire to come here, to make yet another pilgrimage to the shrine of the Mother of Christ, the Mother of the Church, the Queen of Peace.
>
> I am here as a pilgrim, a sign of the pilgrim church throughout the world participating, through my presence as Peter's successor, in a very special way in the centenary celebration of this shrine.

'Blessed art thou among women, and blessed is the fruit of thy womb.' This is also my greeting to *Muire Máthair Dé,* Mary the Mother of God, Queen of Ireland, at this shrine of Knock. With these words, I want to express the immense joy and gratitude that fills my heart today at this place. I would not have wanted it any differently.

Today I come here because I want all of you to know that my devotion to Mary unites me, in a very special way, with the people of Ireland.

An ancient legend tells of the Angel Gabriel, after the Annunciation, showering Mary with half-blown roses as he left. In King's College Chapel, Cambridge, Brother John, a 16th century master craftsman was hired to carve the roses. Aware of the quarrel between King Henry VIII and the Pope, he carved a tiny head of Mary, half-hidden within the petals of a rose. 'There you remain, Our Lady of the Rose, even if wicked men try to drive you and your Son from this church.' When the chapel was stripped of all its association with the old religion, the miniature carved head of Mary remained.

But the most beautiful of all human associations of the rose with Mary are the Rose Windows that brought cathedrals like Chartres to the pitch of perfection. There they remain, great circular gardens of glass, light and colour, symbolising Mary, the Mystical Rose, who continues to show us the Blessed Fruit of her Womb, Jesus.

12. The Black Virgins

Few Christians know that hundreds of European icons of Mary have black faces and black hands. In France they are called *Vierges Noires* or Black Virgins. Elsewhere they are known as Black Madonnas.

A Black Madonna is only surprising because we are familiar with white-skinned Madonnas, just as we are used to picturing Mary clad in sapphire blue, the colour of sea and sky. She is unlikely to have worn blue, seeing she was the wife and mother of poor village carpenters. Moreover, she is mostly depicted as being far too young to have a 33-year-old son.

Mary and Jesus were from a dark-skinned Semitic people. Travel to the sunburned Middle East today and you are unlikely to find a woman as white as our Madonnas.

Mary's dark image is scattered across Europe in hundreds of places. All the Black Madonnas of the 11th and 12th centuries were housed in Catholic churches and cathedrals. The Black Mother with her Black Child is very popular. More candles are lit, more prayer notes left before them than any other statues.

This Virgin attracts millions around the world. Her sacred sites are fascinating, being high on mountains, in caves or beside running water.

France has more than 300 Black Virgin sites, with over 150 Black Virgins still in existence, though some have been 'restored' in white.

The cathedral of Chartres goes back to the 4th century when a church was built around the black figure of a mother giving birth. Many churches replaced it on the same site till the present cathedral was consecrated in 1260.

The black statue of Our Lady Below-Ground in the crypt of Chartes is modelled after the figure honoured by the druids. The original black statue of Our Lady of the Pillar in the upper church, was from the 13th century. During the French Revolution it was destroyed and replaced in 1856 by the present dark wooden sculpture.

The best known Black Madonna is housed at Montserrat, 50 kilometres east of Barcelona. At 700 metres above sea-level, Montserrat – Jagged Mountain – towers over an inky gorge and is surrounded by teeth-like rocky peaks. The journey prepares you for something magical. These days, you can drive along an asphalt road or take the cable car as far the gorge just below the monastery. But the old pilgrims' path, the *camin de l'angel* or Angel's Way, is the best. Beginning near the last spring in the old village at the foot of the mountain, it winds its way for several kilometres with panoramic views along the route, though the monastery is hidden for a long while by mountain crags.

From 1200, miracle stories centring on the new black statue began to circulate in Western Europe. They inspired a famous song cycle in the ancient Galician-Portuguese language, the *Cantigas de Santa Maria* or Songs of Our Lady. In one song, the Madonna comes to the aid of an old shepherdess who had been cheated out of her cash and her flock by a young man. Another describes how she moved a spring from the land of a greedy knight to the garden of thirsty monks. Others relate how the Black Madonna of Montserrat, tenderly referred to as *La Moreneta*, Little Dark One, saved pilgrims and protected monks and the church itself from theft and destruction.

Ever more pilgrims came to praise her or seek pardon for their sins. In time, Montserrat became a place of pilgrimage in its own right and not merely as a stepping stone to the greater *Santiago de Compostela*, 'where the world came to an end'. At the height of its fame, churches as far away as Mexico and Peru were named after the Virgin of Montserrat. The rich brightly coloured garments adorning the wooden statue stress her role as spiritual Mother-Queen of the Middle Ages.

But who is the Black Virgin? Scholars disagree. Some say she was once a goddess of a dark skinned people. From pre-Christian times, people travelled to her shrines to explore her mysteries and beg her to heal, transform and inspire them. Some called her 'the other Mary'.

Many goddesses were pictured as black. If they were absent too long, the earth would be for ever wintry and black, with never a green mantle of spring and summer.

Among the black goddesses were Artemis of Ephesus, Ceres, goddess of agriculture and, most notably, Isis, the

Egyptian Earth Mother. Isis was 'Queen of the Wheatfield', the one 'who gives birth to the fruits of the earth'. Calm and stately, she is often shown suckling her divine baby son, Horus, the Saviour of Mankind. She was prayed to by sailors as the Star of the Sea.

One ancient statue to her bears the inscription:

I am that which is,
has been and shall be.
My veil no one has lifted.
The fruit I bore was the Sun.

Gregory the Great in 601 ordered priests to baptise pagan ideas and practices. The church is at its best when it takes elements from pre-Christian religions and adapts them for its own purposes.

The church was surely wise to cherish the Black Virgins of antiquity. It kept these figures of the Eternal Womanly and christianised them in Mary, the Mother figure of the faith. This is why pope after pope went as pilgrims to venerate them.

The Black Madonnas continue the ages-old tradition of Mother and Child in black stone, usually basalt. Women are the primeval life-force. This begins in darkness, earth darkness, in a womb darkness as black as grave-darkness. Every flower, tree, animal is fashioned in and comes out of darkness, in the case of a human child from the dark of the mother's womb.

But how in fact did Mary become identified with the Black

Virgins? Perhaps through words in the Song of Songs, 'I am black but beautiful.' In the Bible, black means sad, so that to Christians the Black Madonna is Mary, sad and beautiful, weeping over the sins of the world.

Certainly, many of France's Black Madonnas date from the Crusades. St Bernard of Clairvaux visited many shrines of the Black Virgins and wrote commentaries on the Song of Songs, comparing the soul to the bride. Mary was supremely the symbol of the church, the Bride of Christ.

Blackness sometimes suited Mary because it represents her under-earth or winter aspect, not only the earth when green and fertile but also in winter when the soil is dark, still, dormant. If she were to stay away too long the world itself would become wintry and die.

Maybe Mary became the Black Madonna to prove she is both Virgin and Mother, moon and sun, empty and full, fallow and fertile. In the Black Madonna, we celebrate the mystery of the cycles of the seasons, recognising the paradox that change is a constant of time.

The Black Madonna reminds us, too, that Mary is with us always, as much in sorrow as in joy, in times of hunger as well as plenty, in winter as in spring, when we are healthy and when we are sick, when we are dying and when we are at our peak.

To complete the picture, we should remember another simpler source of Europe's Black Madonnas. The dark-skinned people who preceded the Spaniards on the Iberian peninsula depicted Mary as black, seeing that their most beautiful women were black. Later still, when the Moors invaded Spain, the locals preserved their Madonnas in secret caves where the paints and vegetable dyes of the white Madonnas also turned dark over the years.

In the 16th century, the various Black Madonnas were providentially taken to the New World where the people revered them. It filled them with pride to think that Mary and her Son had the same skin colour as themselves. The Black Christ of Esquipulas, Guatemala, and Our Lady of Guadalupe, Mexico, arose out of the conviction that Jesus and the Madonna belonged as much to them as to Europeans.

In recent times, immigrants from Central America brought these black images into the United States where they are poignant reminders of home. To celebrate cultural diversity, several New York churches, for instance in Queens and Brooklyn, have black Christs and black Madonnas alongside the traditional white icons. They are a reminder that Jesus and Mary belong equally to everyone.

PART TWO

Reflections

13. Mary is not a Goddess

Mary's popularity, far from waning, continues to grow. Our Lady of Guadalupe, Mexico, draws 23 million visitors a year; Lourdes, France, 7 million; Poland's Black Madonna, 6 million; Fatima, Portugal, 5.5 million. And there are literally hundreds of other sites. For instance, Knock in County Mayo has 1.5 million visitors each year, more than Dublin's Zoo and Guinness Brewery combined.

As soon as someone claims to have seen the Virgin – in the sky, in the windows of a building, on the roof of a house, on the dome of a church, whether it be in Ireland, the USA, India, Egypt, Poland, Japan, Bangladesh – thousands flock to see it.

In September 2000, John Paul II called for healthy prudence in these matters. He advised the faithful to overcome 'every form of superstition and vain credulity' by listening to church authorities. Yet, he admitted, Mary continues to communicate her message of love, sometimes in surprising ways.

As an example of this, in December 1996, a client of the Seminole Finance Corporation in Tampa Bay, Florida, saw in outline a 30-foot-tall likeness of the classic paintings of a hooded Madonna. On the south wall's three-story glass windows, Mary seemed to be hand-painted in a rainbow of iridescent hues. Thousands turned up to look at it. Among them a local resident, Jim Cascio. He noticed a young woman gazing at the image. 'She was out there for the longest time,' he said, 'alone, crying. She just kept crying. I finally went out there. She told me she had no family. They all had passed away. And now her dog had cancer. And she really felt that this place was helping her. It almost made me cry; I don't know what that thing is, but I don't think it matters any more. It did help people and it does help people.'

Critics have a simple explanation for Mary's continuing popularity: the credulous masses think of her as a goddess.

At first sight, some ancient stories might seem to support this. There is an old tale about a craftsman on a scaffolding high above the nave of a cathedral. Looking down, he saw an old woman praying before a statue of Mary. As a joke, he whispered, hoarsely, 'Woman, this is Jesus speaking.' The woman ignored him so the workman whispered again but louder: 'Woman, this is Jesus.' Still she took no notice. Was she deaf or something? Finally, he cried out, 'Woman, do you not hear me? This is Jesus speaking to you.' The woman raised her eyes to the crucifix above the altar and said, 'Be quiet now, Jesus, I'm talking to your mother.'

The gentle humour of the story makes it plain that Mary is not more important than Jesus though it might be wise sometimes to speak to her first. Gerard Manley Hopkins says Mary 'This one work has to do,/Let all God's glory through.'

While Mary is honoured more than any goddess of old, no Christian believes she is equal to the Father or her divine

Son. Watch when Catholics recite the Rosary. How many times do they bow their head at Mary's name? Never. How many times at the name of Jesus? Always. His name is above all names, that at the name of Jesus every knee shall bow.

The rose is an emblem of silence; everything 'under the rose' or *sub rosa* is secret like sins told in confession. Mary, the Mystic Rose, guarded her silence like a jewel. In the words of John Paul II, she was 'the Virgin of silence and listening'. She worked no miracles. She did not heal the sick, walk on water, still a storm, raise the dead, change water into wine. Like most people, in the world's eyes, she counted for nothing. If she were alive today she would earn the minimum wage.

But her story is too big for Hollywood to handle. Without saying or doing very much, she made history. She became the consoling Mother of the world. Millions of people, as they near their end, remember they have asked her thousands of times to pray for them at the hour of their death.

She became great by pondering God's word in her heart, then putting the God in her arms within our reach.

A simple anonymous Irish poem sees Mary as the mirror of her Lord:

> Love's mirror doubles Love's caress,
> Love's echo to Love's voice is true.
> Their Sire the children love not less,
> Because they love a Mother too.

He, he is King and he alone,
Who lifts that Infant-hand to bless,
Who makes his mother's knee his throne,
Yet rules the starry wilderness.

But was she not conceived immaculate? True, and the Irish were the first to proclaim it. Yet far from proving she was a goddess, this proves she was not. As Pius IX defined this doctrine, Mary was saved by the foreseen merits of her Son. She, like every one of us, was saved – but in a unique way. In the first moment of her existence, Jesus had, in God's design, already died for her. She came to us, as it were, already baptised by his desire.

This is why Christians never need worry about Mary's other titles – even that of mediatrix of all graces – because she is first and foremost saved by her Son. She is entirely of the flesh that perishes like the grass. He alone is the Eternal Word made flesh, the Son of God who emptied himself, taking the form of a servant, freely submitting to death, our death, even the death of the cross.

But is she not also called *Theotokos*, Mother of God? Certainly. But she is not divine. She did not exist before God nor did she make God. Rather, she gave birth to and so humanised the Son of God. The doctrine of Mother of God is not about her divinity but about her Son's.

The Son of God became man, he did not pretend to. He became one of us. If Mary is not God's mother, who did she give birth to? Who died on the cross for us?

Jesus was not a man as well as Son of God. This man was Son of God. Mary was not just the mother of the man, Jesus, as if he could be divided up into man and Son of God. Since he is one person, as Mother of Jesus she is Mother of God.

Christianity is not a message or a doctrine, it is a person. Whoever is associated with him is important, his Mother above all. Her Yes to Gabriel was the moment when the Eternal Word was conceived. That was the beginning of the incarnation and our salvation.

Though Mary is not divine, the incarnation was not possible without her. Someone had to bear God, wash him, feed him, put him to sleep, encourage him, console him. At the Annunciation, she became God's dwelling place, her lap was his throne, her breasts, like any mother's, fed and comforted from birth to death.

It may surprise some that Mary's breasts were praised in medieval times.

> Sweeter those breast of thine
> Than any wine.
> Never was milk so white,
> Lilies were never so bright,
> No flowers or balsam wood
> Ever gave or ever could
> A scent so fine.

But her breasts were praised chiefly because they showed Mary's power to help us. After all, her milk kept alive Jesus, the Son of God. How can Jesus refuse her anything when, as a child, she was his all?

Many poems have Mary saying to Jesus:

> My dear sweet Son, behold the breast,
> With which I fed thee and gave thee rest.

In some, Mary asks her child to forgive her for having no warm clothes for him.

> Jesus, be not angry with me, Sweet,
> For not covering thy little arms and feet,
> For not having wool to thee enfold.
> But now, pretty Babe, as I lay thee to rest
> Press thy tiny feet into my breast
> And let it keep thee from the cold.

In infancy, Jesus looked up to the heaven of her face. In death he looked down on her for strength to endure, for she was proof of what his grace had already done.

In the light of what Jesus achieved, Christians were bound to ask, 'What sort of mother produced this sort of Son? Did he even inherit some of his storytelling ability from listening to the tales she told?'

Hildegard of Bingen speaks of a wind blowing from a high mountain. As it passes over wonderful castles and ornamental towers it stirs a tiny feather and makes it fly. The lowly feather gets all its movement from the wind. It shows what God can do through someone who of herself can do nothing.

The wonder of Mary is that she is not a goddess but a human being who lived a life of perfect conformity to God's will. She is a feather lifted by the wind of the Holy Spirit to the heights of heaven.

For poet Caryll Houselander, Mary is 'The Reed of God', empty until the breath of God blows into her, and through her makes his own music.

> The word of God
> is infinite music
> in a little reed.
> It is the sound of a Virgin's heart,
> beating in the solitude of adoration;
> it is a girl's voice
> speaking to an angel,
> answering for the whole world:
> It is the sound of the heart of Christ,
> beating within the Virgin's heart;
> it is the pulse of God,
> timed by the breath of a child.
> The circle of a girl's arms
> has changed the world –
> the round sorrowful world -
> to a cradle for God.

14. Sources of Devotion to Mary

Some might ascribe devotion to Mary to the yearnings of ignorant peasants. Church authorities, unable to suppress their bizarre ideas, approved them to stop the faithful rioting. In fact, devotion to Mary sprang from great theologians like Augustine and Thomas Aquinas meditating on the Bible.

We each have our own Mary. Or, rather, we each choose that aspect of the gospel story in which she figures to help us in our personal needs. Our Lady of Lourdes is a serene figure dressed in blue and white. Our Lady of La Salette was also beautiful but more like a widow. She was sitting desolate on a mountainside in the French Alps, her eyes streaming with tears at the sin of the world.

Jesus wept over his dead friend Lazarus and over Jerusalem, the unrepentant city that he loved. He offered himself as the everlasting victim. He promised he would be for ever hungry and thirsty and, without doubt, sad and weeping in the racked bodies and tormented souls of his disciples. When Paul met him on the road to Damascus, Jesus said, 'Saul, Saul, why are you persecuting me?'

Mary, too, must often have shed tears, especially on Calvary. In recent times, many of her statues have wept – in Puerto Rico, Sicily, Japan, Korea and Brooklyn – as she herself did at La Salette.

Jesus and Mary cannot be unhappy in heaven, yet we feel there is in them and in God the Father a fellowship with suffering humanity and a fount of compassion that corresponds to our bitter tears on earth.

Mary, smiling or weeping, continues to speak to everyone. For example, a painting called 'The Madonna of the Pinks' was valued by Sotheby's at £100,000 until an expert identified it as a Raphael. For several years, it was hung in London's National Gallery. In July 2003, the Gallery tried to get £20 million of lottery money to top up the amount needed to stop it being sold to the Getty Museum in Los Angeles for $50 million.

Painted about 1507 on a close-grained cherrywood panel, the picture is no bigger than a sheet of typing paper. It is in excellent condition, the colours as fresh as when it left the artist's hands. A youthful Virgin is playing with her baby boy. Seated on a cushion in her lap, Jesus stretches out his hands to the carnation pinks she is holding in front of him.

In an effort to win over the lottery-fund managers, the authorities of the Gallery brought the disadvantaged to see the Raphael – foster children, the homeless, young mothers, some of whom were only 14-years-old – to prove that the Madonna is an inspiration to ordinary people. The Gallery's Director said, 'The women can easily relate to it because of their own circumstances.'

The campaign succeeded. The Gallery bought the picture in February 2004 for £35 million, that is, £338,295 per square inch.

In classical art, Mary is always depicted as an icon of holiness. All the Madonnas are beautiful and serene. Looking at them, ordinary people still find a sense of rest from the troubles of the day.

Some take Mary's words, 'Be it done unto me according to thy Word,' to mean they should imitate her obedience. Others prefer to meditate on the *Magnificat* which, according to *The Catechism of the Catholic Church,* is 'the song both of the Mother of God and of the church' (Sect. 2619). Her song brims over with anger at the way the world is tilted against the poor. It is Mary's cry for justice.

> He has shown strength in his arm,
> He has scattered the proud in the conceit of their hearts,
> He has put down the mighty from their seats
> And exalted the humble;
> He has filled the hungry with good things
> And sent the rich away empty.

Here, Mary shows herself to be not only Queen of Poets but successor to the Jewish prophets who sided with orphans and widows against the greedy rich.

This is a Mary who inspires us to challenge injustice. The poor embody Jesus who continues to suffer in them. 'I was hungry,' he said, 'and you gave me to eat, thirsty, and you gave me a drink.' He could have said, 'I had no rights and you gave them to me.'

In the 19th century, an old African-American woman, born in slavery, was forced to see most of her thirteen children sold into slavery, too. Gaining her freedom in 1827, aged 47, she changed her name from Isabella to Sojourner Truth and dedicated her life to getting civil rights for black women. She said, 'We do as much, we eat as much, we want as much.' At one church meeting, she stood up and pointed to the clergyman: 'That little man in black there, he says women can't have as much rights as men, 'cause Christ wasn't a woman! Where did your Christ come from? Where did he? From God and a woman. Man had nothing to do with him.'

In Neil Boyd's *The Hidden Years,* hard-working Mary is compassionate but tough-minded, too. Not exactly the kind of person portrayed in Renaissance art. Her daily life was a grind. In this extract, Jesus returns home after a night of prayer on the mountainside. He is about to enter and break his fast when he hears his mother inside speaking with the widow Anna, a quarrelsome old neighbour. He leaves them to it. Meanwhile:

> Jesus examined the cucumber beds and the vegetables which his mother was always encouraging to grow bigger and bigger. The onions, she said, were hard of hearing.

> Mary was marvellously content. She spread contentment. What was her secret? Jesus had often asked himself that. His conclusion was, she lived fully in each moment. 'There's too much joy in this moment,' she always said, 'to want it to pass on.'

This may even have explained why she was reckoned

the best grape-picker in the district. She went slowly, methodically, contentedly, along the vines, never missing any grape. Never eating one, either. 'Tomorrow's bread has no taste for me,' was another other favourite saying. 'Today's is sweet enough.'

Tomorrow was as far away for her as a hundred years hence. If you look to the future, try to live in it, you only cheat yourself of the present. 'I'm only a poor woman,' she remarked, with a rare touch of irony, 'so I have to make do with today. When I don't like it, I mend it or sew a patch on it, but I can't afford to give it away or swap it for tomorrow. Who knows, there may not be a today waiting for me next sun-up.'

In addition, she was a mother. For mothers, tomorrow comes soon enough. Too soon. She didn't want to hurry anything along when today passes far too quickly already.

Jesus was thinking this while Anna was complaining that her rent was being doubled by the owner, who had recently become a member of the Jerusalem Sanhedrin.

'He needs extra money for his plumage,' Mary managed to slip in.

'What am I to do?' Anna concluded, in a kind of wail. 'Soon I'll have no place to light a fire.'

'Never you mind,' Mary said. 'God will look after you.' It was always 'God's will' or 'God willing' with her.

'But what about that swine of a landlord?'

'He'll get his desserts, don't worry about that, Anna. God is on the slaves' side, isn't he always? The idle rich won't have it their way for ever.'

Jesus paused in his inspection of the disobedient onion patch to smile at his mother's limitless faith.

'They've had it their way for a long time,' Anna protested.

'Too long, I grant you, Anna dear, but not for ever,' Mary insisted. 'The poor will have their day. God will see to that. He'll wipe away the tears of us that cry and make the greedy howl. Doesn't the Book say, he'll hurl the mighty from their thrones.'

'You reckon so?' Anna was dubious, like a peasant who knows that only rents, taxes, yesterday and today are certain, with a big question mark against the rest of today.

'Can't you see it coming?' Mary said, with a lift of the voice. 'The rich coming trembling to the gates of heaven and the blessed God crying, "Off with you, you heathen," and sending them packing without a penny or a piece of pork.'

It was strange how Jesus' gentle, attentive, tolerant mother was famed in the village for her verbal assaults on the rich and powerful of the earth. Many a time someone grabbed him in the street to whisper, 'Your mother would have made a great prophet, Jesus. She could outcurse Jeremiah if she tried.'

The gospels show Mary knew all about the trials of life. In September 2000, Pope John Paul II said, 'Mary totally lived the daily reality of so many families of her time. She experienced poverty, pain, exile, misunderstanding. She travelled our road and has been in solidarity with us in the pilgrimage of faith.'

Her trials began when she had to travel a long way when she was pregnant. Even before Jesus was born he suffered within her. In the end, Mary had no place to give birth to her Son except a stable on a cold night. After that, she knew exile in a foreign land, fear and deprivation.

How Mary, like any mother, would have loved to give her first-born something better but he came, like many babies before and since, at an inconvenient time. Jesus' presence is seldom convenient to his followers.

Then Simeon spoke of a sword that would one day pierce her heart. Mary would already have known that simply by looking into her Son's eyes. An ancient poet said no human expression is as solemn as a baby's.

It was never easy being so close to him who saves the world. She knew he was suffering for her and for widows and orphans, sinners and saints, all of them her children. St Ambrose said to Monica, mother of Augustine, 'It is impossible for the son of so many tears to perish.' According to Léon Bloy, 'Mary's tears are the very blood of Christ shed in a different way.' This is why the faithful, especially those who admit they are sinners, have confidence in her.

Her sorrows mirror her Son's. If there is one thing worse than being crucified, it is having your mother witness it. This is a theme of the 9th century Irish Hermit Songs:

> At the first bird's cry they began to crucify Thee, O
> Swan!
> Because of it never shall lamentation cease.
> It was like day separating from night.
> Ah, cruel was the pain borne by the Body of Mary's
> Son,
> But crueller still to him was the grief
> that for his sake came upon his Mother.

Mary's tears filled the cup of Jesus' agony to the brim, tears that were for all mankind, from Adam till the end of time. To her, above all, his words were addressed, 'Blessed are those who weep, for they will be comforted.'

15. Mother of the Church and the World

It begins very early in a child's life, the visit to the crib to see the Mother and Baby. It continues throughout the year when he or she is allowed to light a candle before Mary's statue in the church. In time, the child makes the Stations of the Cross, notes the sad meeting between Mother and Son on the road to Calvary and when Jesus, taken down from the cross, is laid dead in her arms.

In every language, the diminutive of mother is the first word learned and often the last word spoken. Many a young man or woman dying in war call out for their mother. The bond between mother and child is the strongest of all bonds. She knows her child before it is born, she feels its every movement. She is the baby's whole world, its food and drink. Any mother would lay down her life for her child, without even thinking about it. A child separated from its mother in early years is always longing for her, many spend years looking for her. Small wonder that a mother's love is the measure of all love.

These experiences are integrated into all religions. According to the Buddha, 'As a mother, even at the risk of her life, protects and loves her only child, so let a man cultivate boundless love towards the whole world, unmixed with any feeling of opposing interest. This state of mind is the best in the world.'

The late Bishop Anthony Bloom spoke of Mary as a model parent. Under the cross, he wrote:

> She said nothing. She accepted the death of her son with the same perfect faith and surrender which she had shown when she accepted the Incarnation.
>
> The Mother of God should be for us an image and an example. Throughout the gospel she is the one who allows her Son to go his way, namely, to enter into all the tragedy which is the destiny of the Son of God who became the Son of Man. This is important for us when someone who is dear to us walks into pain, suffering, anguish.

One Woman's Story

An unnamed American woman tells the story of her grandmother, Sarah, whose own mother died when she was three. Sarah was one of five motherless children, the youngest being only 9 months old. Her father, a coal miner from Pennsylvania, worked hard to rear his family on his own.

One day, when Sarah was sad and lonely, she cried to her father that she missed her mommy very much. He handed her a small statue of the Virgin Mary and told her this was her mother now. She should pray to her, share her problems with her, and ask her for guidance.

The Virgin Mary was the only mother Sarah ever knew and was devoted to her until she died in May 1995.

Before going to her wake, her granddaughter went

through the Christmas decorations in the cellar and found a nativity set Sarah had given her years before. She writes: 'I took out the plastic Virgin Mary and brought it to the funeral home and put it in Grandma's casket, so she could have her Mother with her forever.'

John Paul II

This story is echoed in the life of Pope John Paul II. A child's experience of his mother's death is the most devastating anyone could have. Karol Wojtyla, known then as Lolek, was 8 when his mother died.

One of his first poems, written in 1939 when he was 19, was addressed to her. He called it, 'Over This, Your White Grave':

Over this, your white grave
The flowers of life in white
So many years without you
How many have passed out of sight?
Over this, your white grave
Covered for years
There is a stirring in the air
Something uplifting, and like death
Beyond comprehension.
Over this, your white grave
Oh, mother, can such loving cease?
For all his filial adoration, a prayer,
Give her eternal peace.

Lolek's mother had been ill for some time, an eternity for a child. He was at school when she breathed her last but his father was too grief-stricken to run and tell him. He sent a teacher instead. Lolek did not cry before his peers, nor at the funeral. But the poem reveals how devastated he was then and for years afterwards. After the funeral, his father took him on pilgrimage to Jasna Gora, Bright Mountain, the shrine of Mary. His love for the greatest of all mothers fused with that of his birth mother.

'Over This, Your White Grave' was his first and last poem to his earthly mother In a sequence of poems dated 1950, the mother he speaks of is Mary. Often in his writings and sermons, John Paul addresses Mary directly as he addressed his dead mother in the poem.

While Poland has a great devotion to Mary, the Pope's was surely deepened even more by his early loss. Mary took the place of the mother whom he missed.

In his series of poems entitled 'Mother', another voice is heard, that of John, the beloved disciple. As he stood at the foot of the cross, Jesus turned to Mary and said, 'Woman, behold your son.' Then he turned to John: 'Behold your mother.' In the poem, 'John Beseeches Her,' the disciple feels inadequate to the task. In years to come, John says to Mary:

Don't lower the wave of my heart,
it swells to your eyes, mother;
don't alter love, but bring the wave to me
in your translucent hands.
He asked for this.
I am John the fisherman. There isn't much
in me to love.

I feel I am still on that lake shore,
gravel crunching under my feet –
and, suddenly – Him.
You will embrace his mystery in me no more,
yet quietly I spread round your thoughts like myrtle.
And calling you Mother – His wish –
I beseech you: may this word
never grow less for you.
True, it's not easy to measure the meaning
of the words he breathed into us both
so that all earlier love in those words
should be concealed.

John Paul identifies with the Beloved Disciple. Like him, he lost his own mother and inherited Mary. And Mary is reaching out to him as a son, because he is a disciple of Christ. The influence of Mary fills his writings, especially his 2003 encyclical on the Rosary. And, more important, she fills his life. He was convinced that the attempt on his life on 13 May 1981, in St Peter's Square failed because of her. He objectively recalled that day 13 years later:

We all remember that moment during the afternoon when some pistol shots were fired at the Pope, with the intention of killing him. The bullet that passed through his abdomen is now in the shrine of Fatima; his sash, pierced by the bullet is in the shrine of Jasna Gora in Poland. It was a motherly hand that guided the bullet's path, and the agonising Pope, rushed to the Gemelli Clinic, halted at the threshold of death.

In his view, Mary redirected the bullets away from his vital organs. And in so doing she prepared him for his role of suffering for the church in the long years ahead.

St Teresa of Avila

One of St Teresa of Avila's earliest memories was of her mother Beatriz teaching her about the rosary. When Teresa was 13, Beatriz died. She writes in her *Autobiography*, 'In my affliction I went to an image of Our Lady and begged her with many tears to be a mother to me ... and in the end, she has drawn me to herself.'

She turned to Mary whenever life was difficult and especially on every Marian feast. Convinced that Jesus' mother was the key to her life, she joined the Carmelite Order because of its devotion to Mary.

At least two mystical experiences sprang from meditating on the *Magnificat* which she always recited softly in her native Castilian. But her life as a nun was never a bed of roses. Her union with Mary always gave her the grace to pull through.

When she meditated on Jesus' presentation in the temple, Jesus seemed to say to her, 'Do not think that when you see my Mother holding me in her arms, she enjoyed this happiness without grave torment. From the time that Simeon spoke to her of the sword that would pierce her heart, my Father made her see clearly what I would have to suffer.'

Teresa concludes, 'Those who are nearest to Christ our Lord always have the most to suffer: see what his glorious Mother and the apostles had to go through.'

When, at Easter 1571, Teresa experienced the terrible absence of God known as the Dark Night of the Soul, she was consoled by remembering Mary's anguish and loneliness at the foot of the cross. In the darkness, she heard Jesus say, 'On my resurrection, I went to Our Lady who was in great need and I stayed with her a long while because she needed comforting so much.'

The Little Flower

St Thérèse of Lisieux, known as The Little Flower, also lost her mother, Zeline Martin, when she was a child. Her sister Pauline became a second mother to her. But when Pauline entered the Order of Mount Carmel, Thérèse suffered from a serious nervous condition.

On the evening of Easter, her father put in Thérèse's room a statue of The Virgin of the Smile which had consoled his wife in her last days. Very worried, he had a novena of Masses said for Thérèse at Our Lady of Victories in Paris. During the novena, with her sisters around her bed, Thérèse experienced a remarkable recovery. She describes it in her autobiography *Story of a Soul*:

> Marie knelt down near my bed with Léonie and Céline. Turning to the Blessed Virgin and praying with the fervour of a mother begging for the life of her child, Marie obtained what she wanted.

Finding no help on earth, Thérèse had turned to the heavenly Mother, praying her with all her heart to take pity on her. Later, she recalled moving in and out of consciousness. She was dimly aware of her sisters praying beside her bed. Through eyes that were red and feverish, she saw a blue and white figure outlined in a soft white light standing against the darkness of night and seeming to hover in the air. She knew this was a grace given to her by Mary and she was cured. She writes:

> Suddenly, the Blessed Virgin appeared beautiful to me, so beautiful that never had I seen anything so lovely. Her face was full of an unspeakable kindness and tenderness. But what affected me deep down into my soul was the ravishing smile of the Blessed Virgin.

From then on, Thérèse saw Mary's humble life in Nazareth as the pattern of the Little Way of following Christ, the way of spiritual childhood. In her poem, 'Why I love thee, Mary,' she wrote: 'No raptures, miracles, ecstasies/ Embellish your life,/ O Queen of the elect.' On the contrary, Mary had lived in silence, doing the small things asked of her perfectly, and pondering God's words in her heart.

Eventually, the statue of the Virgin of the Smile came to the Carmel of Lisieux which Thérèse had entered at the age of 17. She prayed before it before she started her autobiography, and all through her terrible trial of faith. She tries to convey in a poem why she loved Mary so much.

> You who smiled on me
> at the dawn of my life
> Come, Mother, smile on me again –
> Now that evening is nigh.

During her final illness, her Carmelite sisters moved the statue of the Virgin of the Smile into the infirmary, at the foot of Thérèse's bed. 'My good Blessed Virgin,' she said, 'this is what makes me most want to leave. I tire out my little sisters, and then I give them pain when being so sick. Yes, I would like to go.'

In the evening of 30 September 1897, she stretched her arms out crosswise and, with her eyes fixed on an image of our Lady of Mount Carmel, she said to the prioress, 'Present me to Our Lady, quickly, and get me ready to die well.'

Still she lingered on. She sighed, 'I would never have believed it possible to suffer so much … I can't breathe and I can't die.' She renewed her readiness to suffer for as long as God and Our Lady wanted her to.

When the Angelus rang at six, she looked up at the smiling Madonna and murmured, 'O my good Blessed Virgin, come to my help.' When she closed her eyes in death it was 7.20 in the evening. She was twenty-four years and nine months old.

Mary had been a good and faithful mother to her.

16. Cardinal Newman's Teaching on Mary

A bowed, white-haired old priest with sight too weak to say his breviary, was never without a Rosary in his hand. John Henry Newman, a cardinal now, was the greatest Christian scholar of the 19th century and a Catholic convert.

In 1832, while still an Anglican and, therefore, not free to pray to Mary, he said:

> In her the destinies of the world were to be reversed, and the serpent's head bruised. On her was bestowed the greatest honour ever put upon any individual of our fallen race … Who can estimate the holiness and perfection of her, who was chosen to be the Mother of Christ? What must have been her gifts, who was chosen to be the only near earthly relative of the Son of God, the only one whom he was bound by nature to revere and look up to; the one appointed to train and educate him, to instruct him day by day, as he grew in wisdom and in stature?

At the end of the 1st century, the martyr Ignatius of Antioch had already said, 'Our God was carried in the womb of Mary,' and many Fathers had used the phrase, 'Death by Eve, life by Mary.' Newman concluded, 'God is her Son, as truly as any one of us is the son of his own mother.' He went on:

> When once we have mastered the idea that Mary bore,

suckled, and handled the Eternal in the form of a child, what limit is conceivable to the rush of thoughts which such a doctrine involves?

Far from Mary being a goddess, she safeguards Christ's divinity. 'Son and Mother went together. Catholics who have honoured the Mother, still worship the Son, while (some) Protestants, who now have ceased to confess the Son, began then by scoffing at the Mother.'

God must have anticipated how people would react at seeing such a humble person raised so high. If God had not meant her to exert that wonderful influence in his church, he himself has misled us. 'If she is not to attract our homage, why did he make her solitary in her greatness amid his vast creation?'

Mary has a natural claim on our hearts in that she is nothing else than our fellow. We look at her without any fear or remorse or the sense that she is able to read us, judge us, punish us.

Of course, while the faith is the same everywhere, private devotion is allowed a certain latitude.

What mother, what husband or wife, what youth or maiden in love, but says a thousand foolish things, in the way of endearment, which the speaker would be sorry for strangers to hear; yet they are not on that account unwelcome to the parties to whom they are addressed. Sometimes by bad luck they are written down, sometimes they get into the newspapers; and what might be even graceful, when it was fresh from the heart, and interpreted by the voice and the countenance, presents but a melancholy exhibition when served up cold for the public eye. So it is with devotional feelings. When (devotion) is formalised into meditations and exercises, it is as repulsive as love-letters in a police report.

Newman's teaching matches that of Simon Grignion de Montfort. Jesus is our Mediator with God the Father. 'But have we no need of a mediator with the Mediator himself? Is our purity great enough to unite us directly to him, and by ourselves?'

Newman also echoed the praises of the Greek Fathers. Mary is 'Morning star, mother of all living, mother of life itself.' This is why her prayer for us never fails. One Greek Father wrote: 'Mary mediates between God and man. She shines out above as the sun above the stars.' Another said, 'Mary is the golden altar of holocaust, God's only bridge to man. Run through all creation in your thoughts and see if there be equal or greater than the Holy Virgin, Mother of God.'

But whereas Jesus died in public view, Mary, the lily of Eden, who had always dwelt out of sight of man, fittingly died 'in the garden's shade, and amid the sweet flowers in which she had lived. Her departure made no noise in the world.'

Newman continues, 'If the Creator comes on earth in the form of a servant and a creature, why may not his Mother rise to be the Queen of Heaven, and be clothed with the sun, and have the moon under her feet?'

Surely, she who had provided God with a human body, should not know decay. 'Why should she share the curse of Adam, who had no share in his fall?' Without the Assumption, Catholic doctrine would be incomplete.

In the last years of Newman's life, the Rosary more than made up for the breviary.

> The great power of the Rosary lies in this, that it makes the Creed into a prayer. It gives us the great truths of Christ's life and death to meditate upon, and brings them nearer to our hearts. The special virtue of the Rosary lies in the way in which it looks at these mysteries. For with all our thoughts of him are mingled thoughts of his Mother. And in the relations between Mother and Son we have set before us the Holy Family, the home in which God lived. Now the family is, even humanly considered, a sacred thing; how much more the family bound together by supernatural ties, and, above all, that in which God dwelt with his Blessed Mother.

In his 'Dream of Gerontius' which Sir Edward Elgar put to music, Newman revealed that at his death, Mary's name would be linked to Jesus'.

> JESU, MARIA – I am near to death,
> And thou art calling me; I know it now.
> Not by the token of this faltering breath,
> This chill at heart, this dampness on my brow –
> (Jesu, have mercy! Mary, pray for me!)

17. Mary in non-Catholic Writings

After making a pilgrimage to Our Lady of Walsingham, Rowan Williams, the Archbishop of Canterbury, wrote a small book, *Ponder These Things: Praying with Icons of the Virgin* (2003). It led some evangelical Anglicans to accuse him of idolatry and popish practices. But Dr Williams regards ancient icons as an invitation to prayer. Standing on the boundary between the spiritual and the everyday, they help us catch the occasional lightning-flash, the revolution in our thinking that enables us to change in order to become more Christ-like.

Russian Orthodox Bishop Anthony Bloom represents the Eastern Church which coined the title Mother of God and pioneered devotion to Mary.

> Take the image of a sail on a sailing ship. The sail is the frailest part of it and yet, directed in the right way, it can engulf the wind and carry the heavy, strong, resisting structure to its haven. This is the kind of weakness, of frailty, of surrender, that we can see in the generous gift of the Mother of God to her Lord. She is the one who is the response of the whole creation to the maker. God offering himself, the creation in her person, accepting him, receiving him, worshipping and lovingly, freely and daringly.

John Paul II caused a surprise in 1999 when he received a

group of Mullahs and, out of respect, kissed the pages of the Koran. He knew that there are more references in the Koran to Maryam, the Virgin Mary, than in the New Testament. Muslims sometimes criticise the Anglican Church for not honouring her enough.

In the Koran's account of the Annunciation, the Angel Gabriel says to the Virgin: 'I am only a messenger from thy Lord,/ To announce to thee the gift of a holy Son.'

For the Prophet, peace be upon him, Mary was the holiest and most marvellous of women. Having reached the summit of servanthood (*ubuda*), she was the best example of the life-giving power of selfless adoration of God. 'Paradise,' he said, 'is at the feet of the Mother.'

There is a story that when Mohammed entered Mecca to cleanse the Kaaba of unworthy images, he left unharmed a fresco of the Virgin and Child.

The Sufi poet Rumi, the most widely read poet in America, wrote 400 songs in Mary's honour and Hajja Muhibba, a 14th century Sufi, wrote in her book, *The Way Of Mary:*

> As many roads to God there are
> As his children have breaths,
> But, of all the roads to God,
> Mary's Way
> is the sweetest and the gentlest.

In the West, after the 16th century Reformation, many Protestants stopped honouring Mary. Shrines were levelled, thousands of stained glass widows broken, statues of

Mary smashed, pictures of the Madonna burnt. In the 17th century, the witty Anglican bishop of Norwich, Richard Corbett, pointed out that even the fairy rings and roundelays and much of the fun had disappeared from the old English countryside.

> By which we note the fairies
> Were of the old profession,
> Their song were Ave Maries,
> Their dances were procession.

One story in particular illustrates the break with the past. The royal palace of Westminster originally belonged to the Kings of England. Next to it was the royal chapel of St Stephen to which was annexed a smaller chapel called Our Lady of the Pew. When the palace became the seat of Parliament under Henry VIII's son Edward VI, the paintings on the chapel walls were covered over with oak panels and the chapels became part of the debating chamber.

In 1800, when the Act of Union united the English and Irish Parliaments, the chamber had to be altered. In the process, the panelling was removed from the walls of the former Marian chapel. The paintings underneath were as fresh as when they were painted 450 years earlier in the reign of Edward III.

Behind the Speaker's Chair was a picture of the Virgin and Child. Acolytes with lighted candles and two angels were in attendance. St Joseph was bending over Mother and Child while Edward III, his Queen, his sons and daughters made an offering to Our Lady.

The picture represents the consecration of England to the Blessed Virgin. Every king and noble approved this consecration until Edward VI.

American writer George Santayana suggests in his *Little Essays* that Catholic devotion to Mary springs from two sources, the incarnation and the crucifixion.

> The figure of the Virgin, found in these mighty scenes, is gradually clarified and developed, until we come to the thought on the one hand of her freedom from original sin, and on the other to that of her universal maternity. We thus attain to the conception of one of the noblest of conceivable roles and of one of the most beautiful of characters. It is a pity that a foolish iconoclasm should so long have deprived the Protestant mind of the contemplation of this ideal.

Not all Protestants dismissed the Catholic ideal of Mary. Probably the most frequently quoted line about Mary is William Wordsworth's. In his 'Hymn to the Virgin', he refers to her as 'Our tainted nature's solitary boast.'

His friend, Coleridge, writes in 'The Rhyme of the Ancient Mariner':

> To Mary Queen the praise be given
> She sent the gentle sleep from heaven
> That slid into my soul.

John Milton's long poem 'On the Morning of Christ's Nativity' begins:

This the month, and this the happy morn,
Wherein the Son of heaven's Eternal King,
Of wedded maid and virgin mother born,
Our great redemption from above did bring;
For so the holy sages once did sing,
That he our deadly forfeit should release,
And with his Father work us a perpetual peace.

For John Donne, Mary provided Jesus with the weakness without which he could not have become one of us or saved us:

Immensity cloistered in thy dear womb,
Now leaves his well-beloved imprisonment,
There he hath made himself to his intent
Weak enough, now into our world to come.

In William Blake's 'Songs of Innocence', there is a cradle song. The Maker, in becoming Mary's child, left his image on the face of every babe. He has wept and smiled for all of them.

Sweet babe, in thy face
Holy image I can trace;
Sweet babe, once like thee
Thy Maker lay, and wept for me:
Wept for me, for thee, for all,
When he was an infant small.
Thou his image ever see,
Heavenly face that smiles on thee!
Smiles on thee, on me, on all,
Who became an infant small;

Infant smiles are his own smiles;
Heaven and earth to peace beguiles.

The favourite poem of many Catholics is 'Hymn' written by the master of the macabre, Edgar Allen Poe:

Sancta Maria! turn thine eyes
Upon the sinner's sacrifice
Of fervent prayer and humble love,
From thy holy throne above.

At morn, at noon, at twilight dim
Maria! thou hast heard my hymn.
In joy and woe, in good and ill
Mother of God! be with us still.

When my hours flew gently by,
And no storms were in the sky,
My soul, lest it should truant be –
Thy love did guide to thine and thee.

Now, when clouds of Fate o'ercast
All my Present, and my Past,
Let my Future radiant shine
With sweet hopes of thee and thine.

Charles Lamb and his sister Mary paid a visit the National Gallery in London's Trafalgar Square. They particularly admired Leonardo's painting 'The Virgin of the Rocks'. Afterwards, Charles wrote this poem:

Maternal lady with the virgin grace,
Heaven-born thy Jesus seemeth sure,
And thou a virgin pure.

Lady most perfect, when thy sinless face
Men look upon, they wish to be
A Catholic, Madonna fair, to worship thee.

In Scots Gaelic, the Virgin Mary is known as *Mathair Uain ghil,* 'Mother of the White Lamb,' and the Golden-Haired Virgin Shepherdess. The next verse, addressed to Jesus, is from 'The Holy Thing' by Scottish minister and poet, George Macdonald.

They all were looking for a king
To slay their foes and lift them high:
Thou cam'st, a little baby thing
That made a woman cry.

Few Marian poems are lovelier that this by Christina Rossetti (1830-1894):

Herself a rose, who bore the Rose,
She bore the Rose and felt its thorn.
All loveliness new-born
Took on her bosom its repose,
And slept and woke there night and morn.
Lily herself, she bore the one
Fair Lily; sweeter, whiter, far
Than she or others are:
The Sun of Righteousness her Son,
She was his morning star.
She gracious, he essential Grace,
He was the Fountain, she the rill:
Her goodness to fulfil
And gladness, with proportioned pace

He led her steps thro' good and ill.
Christ's mirror she of grace and love,
Of beauty and of life and death:
By hope and love and faith
Transfigured to his likeness, 'Dove,
Spouse, Sister, Mother,' Jesus saith.

Josiah Gilbert Holland (1819-1881) wrote this popular poem:

There's a song in the air!
There's a star in the sky!
There's a mother's deep prayer
And a baby's low cry!
And the star rains its fire while the Beautiful sing,
For the manger of Bethlehem cradles a king.

There's a tumult of joy
O'er the wonderful birth,
For the virgin's sweet boy
Is the Lord of the earth.
Ay! the star rains its fire and the Beautiful sing,
For the manger of Bethlehem cradles a king.

In the light of that star
Lie the ages impearled;
And that song from afar
Has swept over the world.
Every hearth is aflame, and the Beautiful sing
In the homes of the nations that Jesus is King.

We rejoice in the light,
And we echo the song

That comes down through the night
From the heavenly throng.
Ay! we shout to the lovely evangel they bring,
And we greet in his cradle our Saviour and King.

In the middle of the lagoon between Venice and the
mouths of the River Brenta there once stood a small shrine
honouring Mary. Standing on rotting wooden piles, it was
called *La Madonna dell'Acque,* the Madonna of the Waters.
No gondolier ever passed the shrine without uttering a
prayer to the Mother of God. In 1844, art critic John
Ruskin was 25 years-old when he wrote a poem to com-
memorate this ancient practice:

Around her shrine no earthly blossoms blow,
No footsteps fret the pathway to and fro;
No sign nor record of departed prayer,
Print of the stone, nor echo of the air;
Worn by the lip, nor wearied by the knee –
Only a deeper silence of the sea …
Oh! lone Madonna – angel of the deep –
When the night falls and deadly winds are loud,
Will not thy love be with us while we keep
Our watch upon the waters, and the gaze
Of thy soft eyes, that slumber not, nor sleep?

In the 20th century, T. S. Eliot writes in 'The Dry Salvages'
of a seaside shrine of Mary. She sympathises with all
women, especially those who await their men who have
gone to war and whom they fear they will never see again.
The poet asks Mary to stand by the side of all women

whose men are lost at sea beyond the ships' bells which the sea's swell turns into an ever-ringing Angelus.

One poem comes from an unlikely source. Field Marshal Lord Wavell wrote it in the midst of war, April 1943. On leave from the Front, this was his response on seeing again a picture, Our Lady of the Cherries, hanging in his family home:

Dear Lady of the Cherries, cool, serene,
Untroubled by our follies, strife and fears.
Clad in soft reds and blues and mantle green,
Your memory has been with me all these years.

Long years of battle, bitterness and waste,
Dry years of sun and dust and Eastern skies,
Hard years of ceaseless struggle for power and hate and lies.

Your red-gold hair, your slowly smiling face,
For pride in your dear son, your King of Kings,
Fruits of the kindly earth, and truth and grace,
Colour and light, and all warm lovely things –

For all that loveliness, that warmth, that light,
Blessed Madonna, I go back to fight.

From the 12th century, Mary's role was revolutionary: she raised respect for women, reversing centuries in which they seemed morally inferior to men. Here was a woman superior to all men fathered by men. Irish historian, W. E. H. Lecky, a consistent critic of the Roman Church, wrote in his *History of Rationalism in Europe*:

Seldom or never has there been an ideal which has exer-

cised a more profound and, on the whole, a more salutary
influence than the medieval conception of the Virgin.

For the first time woman was elevated to her rightful
position. Into a harsh and ignorant and benighted age
this ideal type infused a conception of gentleness and
purity unknown to the proudest generations of the past.

In the sense of honour, in the chivalrous respect, in the
softening of manners, in the refinement of tastes … and
in many other ways, we detect its influence: all that is
best in Europe clustered around it, and it is the origin of
many of the purest elements in civilisation.

Lecky's words are confirmed by Ibn Jubayr, a pious Moor
from an Arab family long settled in Spain. In 1183 he left
Granada on a two-year pilgrimage to Mecca. From Mecca,
he went north to Syria, then in Crusaders's hands. At Acre,
he was incensed to find it full of refuse and excrement and,
worse, of pigs (Christians) and crosses. But further north at
the port of Tyre, he stumbled across a Christian wedding.

A crowd of ornately clad men and women formed two
lines at the bride's door outside of which musical instruments were played until she proudly emerged between two
kinsmen. She wore a beautiful dress with a long train of
golden silk and on her head was a golden diadem covered
by a net of woven gold. 'Proud she was in her ornaments
and dress,' writes Ibn Jubayr, 'walking with little steps like
a dove, or in the manner of a wisp of cloud. God protect
us from the seduction of the sight.'

The seduction consisted in this: the splendid nuptial display proved that a Christian woman was worthy to be the one and only bride of a Christian man. A woman is not a man's possession or plaything but his equal and exclusive partner till death do them part. In the beauty of that celebration in Tyre, Ibn Jubayr feared for the male domination of his own religion in which a man could take four wives and dismiss any of them whenever he wished.

Mary, devoted mother and spouse, so influenced Western thought, there was no question of a man taking more than one wife. That minimum of dignity afforded women was the basis of all their progress, slow and incomplete as it still is, in the ages that followed. Christian men simply cannot discard their wives as still happens in many societies and religions. In Christian culture, any woman is as much a person as any man, and, in many ways, his superior.

In 1909, an English Catholic firm published a book of poetry by an anonymous author, first called *Amphora*, then *Hail Mary*. It received excellent reviews for verses written in Mary's honour like this:

> When Death's cold stream runs black and chill,
> And yew and cypress haunt the hill,
> Be thou our love and comfort still.

Later, the publisher admitted that the poet was an Englishman, Aleister Crowley, known to the media as 'The Wickedest Man in the World' because of his fascination with drugs and the occult. When he died in 1947, his ashes were sent to his followers in the United States.

Mary, it seems, can somehow touch the most troubled soul.

18. Mary and *Uncle Tom's Cabin*

Harriet Beecher Stowe's *Uncle Tom's Cabin, or, Life among the Lowly* was published in 1852. Its sympathetic portrayal of black people created a sensation. Before the Civil War began, it had sold two million copies and during it, Abraham Lincoln greeted her in the White House, with the words, 'So this is the little lady whose book started this big war.' Big, indeed. Over 600,000 Americans died in it.

Harriet referred to herself at this time as 'a little bit of a woman – somewhat more than forty, about as thin and dry as a pinch of snuff.' She felt obliged to speak for the oppressed who could not speak for themselves, for the poor, for women and for black slaves.

'I wrote what I did because as a woman, as a mother I was oppressed and broken-hearted with the sorrows and injustice I saw, because as a Christian I felt the dishonour to Christianity – because as a lover of my country I trembled at the coming day of wrath.'

She was strongly influenced by her mother, Roxanna, who died of consumption when she was five. Her little brother Henry, on being told that their mother had been laid in the ground and had gone to heaven, was found one morning digging in the garden. 'I'm going to heaven to find mamma,' he explained.

Harriet remembered her as 'one of those strong, restful, yet widely sympathetic natures in whom all around seem to find comfort and repose'. Many years later in 1889, when her son Charles proposed to write her biography, she said she wanted it to begin with her mother's death that stayed with her 'as the tenderest, saddest, and most sacred memory' of her childhood.

Harriet's early life in New England was surrounded by death. A one-month-old sister had died three years before she was born and Harriet was given her room, her bedding and her name When she was nine, her little stepbrother Freddy died from scarlet fever. In her married life, she was to suffer even more, losing two of her sons.

On 20 July 1849, cholera struck down her son Samuel. She wrote to her husband who was absent on business: 'Many an anxious night have I held him to my bosom and felt the sorrow and loneliness pass out of me with the touch of his little warm hands. Yet I have just seen him in his death agony, looked on his imploring face when I could not help nor soothe nor do one thing, not one, to mitigate his cruel suffering, do nothing but pray in my anguish that he might die soon.' Of this experience, she wrote, 'It was at his dying bed and at his grave that I learned what a poor slave mother may feel when her child is torn away from her.'

Eight years later, she was to lose another son, aged 19, who was drowned in the Connecticut River

In these tribulations, she seems to have inherited her mother's tenderness. She agreed with her brother Henry Ward

Beecher, 'My mother is to me what the Virgin Mary is to a devout Catholic.' It was a love that enabled her to identify with women, children and black people everywhere.

She found ever more inspiration in the Virgin Mary who, as the mother not only of Christ but of all who suffer, is rightly called the Second Eve.

In her 1859 novel, *The Minister's Wooing,* the female slave Candace takes into her arms Mrs Marvyn who is grieving for her son James. And she rocks her 'as if she had been a babe', all the while reminding her of how Jesus of Nazareth 'looked on his mother' with tenderness. The Saviour knows all about mothers' hearts and he 'won't break yours'.

Another character, Virginie de Frontignac, writes in a letter, 'the bleeding heart of the Mother of God can alone understand such sorrows.'

In 1852, Harriet explained that 'for many years my religious experience perplexed me – I could see no reason for it.' In such confusing times, she could only repeat the words of Mary, 'Behold the handmaid of the Lord.'

If that phrase inspired her acceptance of God's will, the *Magnificat* convinced Harriet that Mary was both poet and prophet. Where did Harriet derive the strength to fight for the emancipation of slaves if not from the lowly woman from Nazareth. Before Jesus said, 'The first will be last and the last first,' Mary had proclaimed, 'God hath put down the mighty from their seat and raised up the lowly. He hath filled the hungry with good things and sent the rich away empty.' The novel 'that started this big war' was inspired by Mary's *Magnificat*. She wanted to show 'what an accursed thing slavery is' with black babies torn from the arms of their slave mothers and their slave fathers forbidden by law to read or write, hold land, make contracts, even get married.

In the front parlour of her home in Hartford, Connecticut, she hung a copy of Raphael's *Madonna of the Goldfinch*, an unusual item in a Calvinist family living in Puritan New England. She also kept copies of at least three other sacred Madonnas, including Raphael's *Madonna del Gran Duca*.

A year after the publication of *Uncle Tom's Cabin*, she went for the first time to Europe. In Dresden, she studied the original of Raphael's *Sistine Madonna*. On her return to the States, she put a copy of it in her home at Andover, Massachusetts. This picture, she said, 'formed a deeper part of my consciousness than any I have yet seen.' In these masterpieces, she saw Mary as 'the crowned queen of women'.

Mary's virginity interested Harriet less than her mother-hood which was a model for all mothers. Mary's maternity extends way beyond the momentous act of giving birth to the Saviour. It includes her role as his teacher and all the quiet years of tending him.

If Jesus lacked a human father, she argued, 'all that was human in him' derived from his mother. This fits in with the gospel picture of Jesus in whom there was 'more of the pure feminine element than in any other man. It was the feminine element exalted and taken in union with divinity.'

In her 1849 poem 'Mary At The Cross', Harriet meditates on
the words of John's gospel, 'Now there stood by the cross of
Jesus his mother.' She begins with the Annunciation:

And then it came, that message from the highest,
Such as to woman ne'er before descended,
The almighty wings thy prayerful soul o'erspread,
And with thy life the Life of worlds was blended.

What visions then of future glory filled thee,
The chosen mother of that King unknown,
Mother fulfiller of all prophecy
Which, through dim ages, wondering seers had shown!

Well, did thy dark eye kindle, thy deep soul
Rise into billows, and thy heart rejoice;
Then woke the poet's fire, the prophet's song,
Tuned with strange burning words thy timid voice.

The poet passes on to the quiet years in Nazareth:

O highly favoured, thou in many an hour
Spent in lone musings with thy wondrous Son,
When thou didst gaze into that glorious eye,
And hold that mighty hand within thine own.

Blest through those thirty years, when in thy dwelling
He lived a God disguised with unknown power;
And thou his sole adorer, his best love,
Trusting, revering, waited for his hour.

On Calvary, the hour struck at last:

Now by that cross thou tak'st thy final station,
And shar'st the last dark trial of thy Son;
Not with weak tears or woman's lamentation,
But with high, silent anguish, like his own.

Hail! highly favoured, even in this deep passion;
Hail! in this bitter anguish thou art blest –
Blest in the holy power with him to suffer
Those deep death-pangs that lead to higher rest.

All now is darkness; and in that deep stillness
The God-Man wrestles with that mighty woe;
Hark to that cry, the rock of ages rending –
'T'is finished!' Mother, all is glory now!

In 1867, Harriet dedicated her poem, 'The Sorrows of Mary,' to mothers who had lost sons in the Civil War, remembering the 'anguish of disappointed hopes'. Since the death of her two sons and, lately, of her two dear brothers, Henry and Charles, she identifies still more closely with Mary of the *stabat mater*: 'Had ye ever a son like Jesus / To give to a death of pain?'

She knew that, being a mother herself, she could not escape Simeon's prophecy, 'And thine own soul a sword shall pierce.' She believed that whether she knows it or not, whether her face be white or black, every grieving mother is the embodiment of the Madonna.

Finally, it is a remarkable fact that through its influence on Harriet Beecher Stowe, Mary's *Magnificat* was largely responsible for the American Civil War and the emancipation of the Negro slaves.

19. Mary and the Great Cathedrals

Impressive testimony to Mary's significance comes from another New England Protestant. Henry Adams (1838-1918) was the great-grandson of John Adams, the second President of the United States, and grandson of Quincy Adams, another US President. Two medieval churches, the Abbey at Mont St Michael and Chartres Cathedral, showed him the tremendous impact Mary made on medieval society and explained her appeal throughout the ages.

Known for the first time in the Middle Ages as Notre Dame, Our Lady, meaning Lady of us all, Mary was part of the European landscape. She was revered in homes and roadside shrines in every town, hamlet, and mountain pass. Church bells reminded the faithful of her. Thousands of holy wells, known as Mary's Wells, were miracles in their way; they never failed even in droughts and were coolest on the hottest days. There, thanksgiving was offered to Mary the healer.

Henry V of England, like other monarchs of the time, wrote in his will that he hoped to reach heaven 'through the prayer of Mary, the High Mother of God'. He paid for 5,000 Masses to be said in her honour on his death. Schools and universities such as Eton and King's College, Cambridge, were put under her protection.

For five centuries, her image was on the mastheads of

ships, on the banners, shields and swords of rival armies, each chanting the *Salve Regina*, loveliest and saddest of hymns, before battling with each other in Mary's name.

But the most formidable witness to her is the eighty cathedrals and five hundred major churches built in France to honour her between 1170 and 1270. Never before or after have such beautiful building been erected in Europe.

Not content with a cathedral, she required 'in all churches a chapel of her own, called in English the Lady Chapel, which was apt to be as large as the church was, but was always meant to be handsomer; and there behind the high altar, in her own private apartment, Mary sat receiving her innumerable suppliants.'

The palaces of earthly queens could not compare with those of the Queen of Heaven. Put them together and treble their size, they could not rival any single cathedral dedicated to Mary.

In today's terms, these churches and cathedrals cost billions; they took up the bulk of the wealth of France at a time when the only profit expected from them was spiritual. That, of course, was the point: heaven was as real to people then as trees and bricks, water and bread.

Of all French cathedrals, Chartres is the oldest, grandest and most representative of its age. It has nearly four thousand carvings and majestic stained-glass windows. Henry Adams called the Rose window 'a jewel so gorgeous that no earthly majesty could bear comparison. Never in 700

years has one looked up at this Rose without feeling it to
be Our Lady's promise of Paradise.' The entire cathedral is
a study in glass and stone of how the Virgin influenced the
whole of medieval life.

She was the compassionate Mother who, Christians
believed, would plead for them, they being too unworthy
to approach Jesus themselves. The workmen and the architects took their orders directly from her. She supervised the
laying of every stone. She was to them a close and living
force.

Adams puts this down to the womanliness of the age. This
was what gave strength, harmony and unity to the works
of faith. The Virgin of Chartres, he explains, is 'gracious
and gentle', the greatest of all Queens, but also the most
womanly of women. The cathedral idealised the feminine.
Only Gothic architecture ever gave 'this effect of flinging
its passion against the sky'.

Being a woman, Mary surrounds herself with light and joy.
Nowhere in her palace are there any 'hints of fear, punishment, or damnation'. Angry at times, she remained a
woman who loved grace and beauty, especially in her robes
and jewels. Chartres showed her to be the supreme artist,
philosopher, musician and theologian. 'The rose windows,'
Adams writes, 'the unusual arrangement of the apses, the
legendary windows – they were planned and executed to
please the personal tastes of the Queen of Heaven.'

The men and women of the 13th century felt that Mary
was one of them. She shared their joys and sorrows,

accepted their weaknesses, begged forgiveness for their sins because she understood human frailty.

In her miracles, they saw her protecting them from the wrath of God. In a striking phrase, Adams says: 'The Virgin embarrassed the Trinity. And perhaps this is the reason why men loved and adored her with a passion such as no other deity has ever inspired. Mary concentrated in herself the whole rebellion of man against fate; the whole protest against divine law.'

Mary defended outcasts and sinners because they, too, were her children, however wayward. 'She cared not a straw for conventional morality, and she had no notion of letting her friends be punished, to the tenth or any other generation, for the sins of their ancestors and the *peccadilloes* of Eve.'

However great Chartres is, what is not seen is even more impressive. The place is still haunted by the men who worked on it. They are not slaves, nor are they all day labourers. The rich, too, bow their necks, dragging like beasts of burden 'wagons, loaded with wines, grains, oil, stone, wood, and all that is necessary for the wants of life, or for the construction of the church'. And though thousands are employed at a time, not a murmur is heard from them. When they halt on the road, the only sound they make is of prayer and the confession of sins.

The church site was a spiritual camp. All night there were hymns, prayers, canticles. Lighted lamps were placed on each wagon for people to bring their sick and have them blessed with the relics of the saints. All begged mercy of the Lord and his Mother for their recovery.

In his autobiography, *The Education of Henry Adams*, he returned to the notion of womanly force embodied in Mary. 'Maternity and reproduction,' he writes, 'are the most typical, uniting history in its only unbroken and unbreakable sequence.'

Western civilisation, centred on Mary, realised 'an intensity of connection never again reached by any passion whether of religion, of patriotism, or of wealth; perhaps never even paralleled by any single economic effort except in war.'

Adams' chapter 'The Dynamo and the Virgin' takes us through the Great Paris Exhibition in 1900. However stupendous it was, it only proved to him that Mary's inspiration had disappeared from the modern world. In its place is the dynamo, the source of electricity, a power as hidden as that of the Madonna in the Middle Ages. But to be used for what? Can you fashion with blind unco-ordinated force the kind of civilisation that faith in Mary forged?

At the Exhibition there was a big forty-foot wheel, very impressive for its time. He recognised that the dynamo was not science undoing mythology but science as the new mythology. People were putting their faith in science as they once put their faith in the church. They didn't understand the technology but they believed in it. Faith in religion was replaced by blind faith in the forces of modern science whose one aim was to make people rich – in this life.

'Symbol or energy,' Adams writes, 'the Virgin had acted as the greatest force the Western world ever felt, and had drawn man's activities to herself more strongly than any other power, natural or supernatural, had ever done.' The power to be gained from electricity and steam is not a moral force. 'All the steam in the world could not, like the Virgin, build Chartres.'

To enjoy Chartres fully, you must for the time believe in Mary and feel her presence as the architects did, in every stone they laid, and obey her in everything. Being in that holy space, 'If you had only the soul of a shrimp, you would crawl to kiss her feet.'

After Adams' death, among his private papers was found a Prayer to the Virgin of Chartres. It expressed the hopes of millions and perhaps his own as well:

> For centuries I brought you all my cares;
> And vexed you with the murmurs of a child;
> You heard the tedious burden of my prayers;
> You could not grant them, but at least you smiled.

20. Mary and Martin Luther

Few Catholics and non-Catholics know that the first of all Protestants, Martin Luther, had a deep, lifelong devotion to Mary. He even kept a picture of her in his study. Many Lutherans are unaware of this. They themselves would never think of praying the Rosary or keeping medals and pictures of Mary.

Luther constantly called Mary *Theotokos,* Mother of God. He also believed in the Immaculate Conception when Catholics were not obliged to believe it and when saints and theologians like Bernard and Thomas Aquinas denied it. Luther's beliefs shines through all his writings. In orthodoxy and warmth of feeling they rank with the finest teaching of Catholic or Orthodox theologians.

> God says: 'Mary's Son is my only Son.' Thus Mary is the Mother of God. God did not derive his divinity from Mary; but it does not follow that it is therefore wrong to say that God was born of Mary, that God is Mary's Son, and that Mary is God's mother. She is the true mother of God and bearer of God. Mary suckled God, rocked God to sleep, prepared broth and soup for God. For God and man are one person, one Christ, one Son, one Jesus, not two Christs, just as your son is not two sons, even though he has two natures, body and soul, the body from you, the soul from God alone.

Mary is the Mother of Jesus and the Mother of all of us even though only Christ reposed on her knees. Where he is, we ought to be. All that he has ought to be ours, and his mother is our mother, too.

We can use the Hail Mary to meditate on the grace that God has given her. We should add a wish that everyone may know and respect her.

In the *Magnificat*, Mary says, 'My soul magnifies the Lord' – that is, my whole life and being, mind and strength, esteem him highly. She is caught up, as it were, into him and feels herself lifted up into his good and gracious will.

The true honour of Mary is the honour of God, the praise of God's grace. She reveals, by word and example, how to know, love, and praise God. Mary is nothing for her own sake, but all for Christ's sake. She does not wish us to come to her, but through her to God.

She teaches all rulers how to rule and shows us the nature of God. May the tender Mother of God procure for me the spirit of wisdom so I may profitably and thoroughly expound this her song.

The veneration of Mary is inscribed in the very depths of the human heart. She is the highest woman and the noblest gem in Christianity after Christ. She is nobility, wisdom, and holiness personified. We can never honour her enough, though honour and praise must be given her in such a way as not to injure Christ or scripture.

She is full of grace and entirely without sin – something exceedingly great. For God's grace fills her with every good thing and empties her of evil. 'No woman is like you, Mary. You are more than Eve or Sarah, blessed above all nobility, wisdom, and sanctity.'

It is a sweet and pious belief that in the infusion of her soul she was purified from original sin and adorned with God's gifts, receiving a pure soul infused by God; thus from the first moment she began to live she was free from all sin.

Christ was the only Son of Mary, and the Virgin bore no children besides him. 'Brothers' really means 'cousins' here, for Holy Writ calls cousins brothers.

Eve brought forth thorns and thistles (that is, evil men and sinners), and mankind did likewise. But Mary brought us the Lily of the Valley, the Rose, the Grape, and the Almond; and through her mankind has brought forth grapes and figs, meaning all good works.

There can be no doubt that the Virgin Mary is in heaven. How it happened we do not know. And since the Holy Spirit has told us nothing about it, we can make of it no article of faith. It is enough to know that she lives in Christ.

The texts force on us an extraordinary conclusion. Luther's teaching on Mary is much closer to Catholicism than to modern-day Lutheranism. One Protestant scholar expresses deep sadness at what happened to Lutherans in the 18th century. 'Church festivals in honour of Mary and everything to do with her were done away with in the Protestant Church. Every biblical relationship to Mother Mary was lost, and we still suffer from this heritage.'

Such words encouraged John Paul II to hope for closer ties between Catholics and Protestants. After all, the Formula of Concord (1577), binding on all Lutherans, reads:

> On account of this personal union and communion of two natures (in Christ), Mary, the most blessed virgin, did not conceive a mere, ordinary human being, but a human being who is truly the Son of the most high God. He demonstrated his divine majesty even in his mother's womb in that he was born of a virgin without violating her virginity. Therefore she is truly the Mother of God and yet remained a virgin.

A final quote from Luther shows how eloquent he was in praising Mary:

> Mary became the Mother of God causing great good things to be bestowed on her such as pass our understanding. Flowing from this are all honour and blessedness. In the whole of mankind, she has no equal for she had a child by the Father in heaven, and such a Child.
>
> This is why men have crowded all her glory into a single name, Mother of God. None can say of her greater things, though he had as many tongues as the earth has flowers and blades of grass, the sky has stars and the seas have grains of sand.

POSTSCRIPT:

Blessed among Women

This book provides a thousand reasons why Mary is blessed among women. It ends with a poem by Gertrude Von Le Fort, 'I Sing Of A Maiden.' It contrasts our emptiness with the blessings Mary bestows:

Your voice speaks:
Little Child out of Eternity,
now will I sing to thy Mother!
The song shall be fair
as dawn-tinted snow.

Rejoice Mary Virgin,
daughter of my earth, sister of my soul,
rejoice, O joy of my joy!
I am as one
who wanders through the night,
but you are a house under stars.
I am a thirsty cup,
but you are God's open sea.

Rejoice Mary Virgin,
blessed are those who call you blessed,
never more shall child of man
lose hope.
I am one love for all,
I shall never cease from saying:
one of you has been exalted by the Lord.

Rejoice Mary Virgin,
wings of my earth,
crown of my soul,
rejoice, joy of my joy!
Blessed are those who call you blessed.

APPENDIX

The Hail Mary in many Languages

To show the catholicity of the angel's greeting to Mary, here is a small selection from the 150 languages in which it is recited every day.

Latin:

Ave Maria, gratia plena, Dominus tecum, benedicta tu in mulieribus, et benedictus fructus ventris tui, Jesus. Sancta Maria, Mater Dei, ora pro nobis peccatoribus, nunc et in hora mortis nostrae. Amen.

English:

Hail Mary, full of grace, the Lord is with thee. Blessed art thou amongst women and blessed is the fruit of thy womb Jesus. Holy Mary, Mother of God, pray for us sinners, now and at the hour of our death. Amen.

Gaelic:

'Sé do bheath' a Mhuire, atá lán de ghrásta, tá an Tiarna leat. Is beannaithe thú idir mná agus is beannaithe toradh do bhruinne Íosa. A Naomh Mhuire, a mháthair Dé, guí orainn na peacaithe, anois is ar uair ár mbás. Amen.

Italian:

Ave Maria, piena di grazia, il Signore è con Te. Tu sei benedetta fra le donne e benedetto è il frutto del tuo seno, Gesù. Santa Maria, madre di Dio prega per noi peccatori, adesso e nell'ora della nostra morte Amen

Spanish:

Dios te salve María, llena eres de gracia, el Señor es contigo, bendita tú eres entre todas las mujeres, y bendito es el fruto de tu vientre, Jesús. Santa María, Madre de Dios, ruega por nosotros pecadores, ahora y en la hora de nuestra muerte. Amén.

Portuguese:

Ave Maria, cheia de graca, o senhor é convosco; bendita sois vós, entre as mulheres, e bendito é o fruto do vosso ventre Jesus. Santa Maria, Mãe de Deus, rogai por nós pecadores, agora e na hora da nossa morte. Amen.

French:

Je vous salue, Marie, pleine de grâces, le Seigneur est avec vous, vous êtes bénie entre toutes les femmes, et Jésus le fruit de vos entrailles est béni. Sainte Marie, Mère de Dieu, priez pour nous pauvres pécheurs, maintenant, et à l'heure de notre mort. Ainsi-soit-il.

German:

Gegrüsst seist du, Maria, voll der Gnade; der Herr ist mit dir; du bist gebenedeit unter den Frauen und gebenedeit ist die Frucht deines Leibes, Jesus. Heilige Maria Mutter Gottes, bitte für uns Sünder, jetzt und in der Stunde unseres Todes. Amen.

Dutch:

Wees gegroet Maria, vol van genade, de Heer is met U, Gij zij de gezegende onder de vrouwen, en gezegend is Jesus, de vrucht van Uw schoot. Heilige Maria, Moeder van God, bidt voor ons zondaars, nu en in het uur van onze dood. Amen.

Cheyenne Indian:

Ave Maria, zenanosheamaesz Maheo zevissevata zeshivata-maet zeoxextohevoxzheeo, na ninanoshivatama nihevetox-eszexaet Jesus. Sana maria Maheo heeshk, nixaona-otshe-men havsivevo-e-tastovez, hezeze namaxoost nanastonan. Enahaan.

Philipino:

Aba Ginoong Maria, Napupuno ka ng grasya. Ang Panginoon ay sumasaiyo. Bukod kang pinagpala sa babaeng lahat, at pinagpala naman ang Iyong anak na si Hesus. Santa Maria, ina ng Diyos, ipanalangin mo kaming makasalanan, ngayon at kung kami'y mamamatay Amen.

Tok Pisin: (Pidgin English, a Creole form of English spoken in Papua New Guinea.)

Ave, Maria, yu pulap long grasia. Lord, i stap long yu. Ol i onaim yu moa long ol meri, na ol i onaim Jisas, Em Pikinini bilong bel bilong yu. Santu Maria, Mama bilong God, pre bilong helpim mipela manmeri bilong sin, nau na long taim milpela i dai. Amen.

Esperanto:

Mi vin salutas, Mario, plena je favoroj, la Sinjora estas kun vi; vi estas benat inter la virinoj, kaj estas benata la frukto de via ventro Jesuo. Sankta Mario, dipatrino, pregu por ni pekuloj, nun kaj en la horo de nia morto. Amen.